D0651986

TRAINED TO KILL

TRAINED TO KILL
SOLDIERS AT WAR

THEODORE NADELSON, M.A., M.D.

Clinical Professor of Psychiatry and Vice Chair
for Education, Boston University School of Medicine

Former Chief of Psychiatry, Boston VA Medical Center

Clinical Professor of Psychiatry, Tufts University
School of Medicine, Boston, Massachusetts

THE JOHNS HOPKINS UNIVERSITY PRESS

BALTIMORE AND LONDON

© 2005 The Johns Hopkins University Press
All rights reserved. Published 2005
Printed in the United States of America on acid-free paper
9 8 7 6 5 4 3 2 1

The Johns Hopkins University Press
2715 North Charles Street
Baltimore, Maryland 21218-4363
www.press.jhu.edu

Library of Congress Cataloging-in-Publication Data

Nadelson, Theodore, 1930–2003.
Trained to kill : soldiers at war / Theodore Nadelson.
    p.   ; cm.
Includes bibliographical references and index.
ISBN 0-8018-8166-8 (hardcover : alk. paper)
1. War and society. 2. War—Psychological aspects—
Case studies. 3. Veterans—Psychology—Case studies.
4. Vietnamese Conflict, 1961–1975—United States.
5. Post-traumatic stress disorder.
[DNLM: 1. Combat Disorders. 2. Men—psychology.
3. Social Values. 4. Violence—psychology. 5. War.
WM 184 N134k 2005] I. Title.
U21.5.N33 2005
355.02'01'9dc22   2004021138

A catalog record for this book is available
from the British Library.

CONTENTS

NOTE TO THE READER

Theodore Nadelson, M.D., had completed this book and was making final edits when he died in October 2003. It was a labor of many years and the culmination of a substantial part of his professional lifetime. It became our task to complete the editing and ensure the book's publication. We have preserved his words and conceptualization, adding a small amount of material that has come to light since his death, confident that he would have done the same. Some references are incomplete because we were unable to locate the specifics of personal interviews, such as dates and circumstances, in his materials. We are grateful for the meticulous reference search performed by Sandra Gould, M.A., M.S.M., and for the patience, intelligence, and support of Wendy Harris, his editor. Had he survived to bring this book to publication, he would most certainly have expressed his enormous gratitude to the many veterans who gave consent for him to reveal their stories. To preserve the confidentiality of those veterans whose words appear here, they are respectfully recognized as they are referenced: D.R., D.K., E.P., O.I., N.S., N.P., R.O., R.M., V.E., A.D., R.T., O.G., S.F., M.B., B., O.T., F.M., C.I., W.B., S.V., P.K., E.B., T.N.P., and R.A.

DON RICHARD LIPSITT, M.D.
CAROL COOPERMAN NADELSON, M.D.
ROBERT ERIK NADELSON, M.A.L.D., J.D.

LeRoy G. Schultz
Emeritus Professor
West Virginia University
Morgantown, WV 26506

PREFACE

I wrote this book after a long march. War has always been a part of my consciousness. It is a part of my history and that of my family, as in most families. As boys growing up before World War II, we played as soldiers. We didn't want sissies and excluded those who could not fit the pattern of group aggression.

Rejection could be savage. At age eight, I was part of a group who went after another boy, the teacher's favorite. We had no reason other than that he was a sweet, soft boy with multiple allergies and asthma that did not allow him to join the rough and tumble. We chased and cornered him against a fence and landed blows, probably not damaging in themselves but hurtful. I remember the feeling of delirious release as we attacked him. Sixty-five years later, I prefer to think that I did not hit him myself—but I'm uncertain, and I know that I might have. The boy had an acute asthmatic attack afterward, and the teachers told us when they punished us that he "could have died." They did not know that we had attacked shouting, "Kill him!"

Like other boys growing up during World War II, I went to the movies avidly, and I still remember the images on the screen with greater clarity than many other aspects of my life. *Wake Island* appeared in 1942 almost on the heels of the Japanese attack on the island. Other movies, such as *The Sands of Iwo Jima*, repeated similar themes: war's urgent necessity and the heroic sacrifice of our soldiers in contrast to the deceptive, cowardly, and cruel behavior of the enemy. What we knew about the War's progress came from newspaper and radio, but our emotional connection to it was through Hollywood images. Filmmakers back then avoided clear pictures of wounds inflicted; on screen, soldiers fell as we did during our play at war. Death did not seem unkind or ugly, and as boys we only half sensed war's savagery and accepted with conviction that war delivered glory.

My father, who had been in the trenches with the 107th Infantry in World War I, told me war stories when I was a child, some of which I gradually realized he had made up, a fiction for the wonder of a boy. With a new world war about to start, he remembered with singular clarity many events of the War twenty years before. His stories of war were a part of my childhood and still are a part of my picture of him. I knew that he wanted me to recognize that he had been a combat soldier. Even though he may not have been dramatically heroic, he had been under fire and available to the possibility of heroism.

When he was tipsy, my father would often sing, to my delight, "I belong to Glasgow, dear ould Glasgow town / There's something the matter with Glasgow, for it's going roun' and roun'"—in an imitation of Harry Lauder's Scottish accent. Lauder was a revered performer and had entertained a gathering of American and British troops at some point in that War, and my father remembered it even to the time of his own death. Years later, when I sang Sir Harry's song to my delighted children, imitating the way my father had sung it, I did it without any awareness of the reason. That reason is the main direction of this book. Drafted at age twenty-one, just out of college in 1951, I was placed in a barracks at Fort Dix, New Jersey, with a group of men similar to me. We thought only about surviving the sixteen weeks of basic infantry training. We knew dimly that the Army was attempting to train us to be capable of killing in Korea, but we kept such thoughts at a distance while we resisted any basic change in ourselves. We shared resentment toward those in charge and toward the Army in general; there was little anger toward the North Korean or People's Republic soldiers. I controlled my terror of the moment when I would be forced to kill or die myself.

It was the bayonet that precipitated my most serious doubt about whether I was ever to be a good enough soldier. We often trained in a fatigued and dissociated state: marches, weapons firing, overhead artillery. Scared, I crawled through an infiltration course criss-crossed with barbed wire, a "no man's land" in a World War I anachronism. These are moments still frozen in memory: machine guns fixed in a traverse so bullets passed just overhead, mines exploding close enough that I was deaf for seconds. At the end, as commanded, I charged, lurched toward a straw-filled enemy, and pushed my wavering bayonet home, accompanied by a required final shout more of exhaustion than of bold determination. I knew I lacked what the cadre called "the spirit of the bayonet." I denied the idea that all of this was directed toward the purpose of killing an Asian male. The instruction we received was focused on victory and our survival but was also meant to prime "a joy of killing" within us—or, if not that, then at least enthusiasm for the use of mortal force. Despite my denial, I vaguely recognized that if I ever faced an armed enemy soldier, I had to be strong in resolve to prevail or I would die. During occasional moments of lucidity, I thought that there was more than a reasonable possibility that the Asian male might kill me because I did not have the stuff for soldiering.

I occasionally worried about my own death but more about not coming up to standard, my defect as a man displayed as I failed my comrades. I wanted to think I could kill if I had to—above all, not be a coward. Because I had never faced an armed enemy, I lacked the absolute assurance that I had passed "the test," but I tried to convince myself that I had come close enough. I assumed that my friends shared some of this feeling, but we never spoke about it.

One man in my company was "a good soldier." Tall, lean, raw looking, and angry, he had enlisted, and his suitability was early recognized by those in charge. Those of us who stayed together as friends had been drafted. We derisively referred to him as "R.A." (for the letters preceding his serial number meaning "regular Army," as opposed to our draftee designation). I still have a strong memory of R.A. shouting, "You motherfuckers will all die" into the blackness of the New Jersey night when we had, again, failed to stay vigilant during an overnight bivouac.

I realized at some point that the Army was trying to train us to survive against a more dangerous and real opponent than it was possible for us to contemplate. Despite our combined resolve not to recognize it, we knew that we would have far less chance of survival than R.A. had, confronting a charge as described by one of our instructors returned from the war: "There were waves, masses of seasoned Chinese Regulars coming at you, down a hill, in quilt coats. It was so fucking cold. We got disorganized, some guys ran, throwing away their sleeping bags, everything, then got killed. The Chinese killed a lot of us. More get killed turning tail than staying. You guys have to know what to do and not spook." We hoped for the miracle that would direct us away from Korea or, with the optimism of youth, that if we were sent, we would suddenly find a way to pass the test and survive.

With shared disrespect for the military and serious concerns about why we were in the War, my friends and I still gained strength and stamina. Together we became leaner and tougher than ever before. The training worked despite our resistance to it. We became a group of comrades. We were dragging under our equipment on a twenty-mile march back to the barracks after an all-night field maneuver when, within a mile of our barracks, we were given the order to straighten up and march to shouted cadence. We grumbled until we caught the rhythm of the march, and then we felt the lift of shared youth and shared aggression. We started to shout the cadence at the top of our lungs. We found out afterward that we all had the same thought: we wanted someone to get in our way so that we could trample him into the ground. The kinesthetic feeling is within grasp of memory; it is still in my body. But I can bring up only its ghost, and the full measure is, I confess, wanted again.

I am far too old now for war, and I reject war reflexively because of fear of its personal and collective consequences. I am a psychiatrist and psychoanalyst with forty years of experience. I have worked at the Boston Veterans Administration Hospital for twenty years with many Vietnam combat veterans who have post-traumatic stress disorder. Their war in Vietnam as told to me stitches together this book.

In my work as a psychiatrist, I listen to veterans' stories of war's constant wonder and terror and of their deepest loyalty toward comrades. After many years, I continue to find their combat narratives compelling. I was surprised when I discovered that in myself. I should not have been.

Theodore Nadelson, M.D.

PART I

BOYS BECOME SOLDIERS

ONE

BOYS

PLAYING AT WAR

We were above a rice paddy, two of us, hunkering down together. We could see Vietcong Regulars, one "klick" [kilometer] out . . . We were low on caps—and, Jesus, we were plenty scared. This kid with me is new, a replacement, and he says, "You know, I just had the thought, like it was only minutes ago, that I was playing soldier, doing this, with the other kids on the block."   —D.R.

It was funny, just then, at that very same time, I was thinking exactly the same thing.   —T. Nadelson

The myth of maleness is a prominent shaper of our culture. The ritual of initiation makes the myth a substantive reality. It distinguishes the acceptable man from the unacceptable. There may be a genetic schematic in which such behavior is favored as adaptive for fitness, but culture clearly shapes and defines its expression, and the myths flourish in both agrarian societies and industrial states.

The characteristics wanted in the soldier are those often disparaged by elders as "childish." In war, the boy's unswerving loyalty to his group, daring, impulsiveness, and lack of concern for the future are the characteristics of the soldier and the exalted hero. The soldier's task in war is driven by absolute immediacies. It is stressful and deadly. It builds on boys' play and contest (Cox 1993).[1] In World War I, British enthusiasts described soldiering as "rough play in the open air" for boys (Winter 1979).

SPORT

Boys focus on the necessary use of aggression early in their games. Competitive play is serious, and boys have dreams in which they rise to the place of the hero through victory—and secure manhood in the winning. The boy of ordinary ability who cannot become a school hero or is otherwise disparaged, wounded by lack of recognition, may try to achieve respect, hurt back, or get notice in some way, even destructively (Gilligan 1996).

All sport is entertainment, but more than entertainment. Sport is not just diverting, it is compelling. It contains the unpredictability of contest, the possibility of the improbable, and the chance that the tables will be turned by resolute action. It is the entertainment that the media routinely present as news.

Professional athletes become models for boys, whether or not they want the role; they are revered because they are adults who play as boys but far exceed normal limits of competence. The professional athletes' world is one of fierce competition, and although they do not face death, as did the athlete-gladiators of Imperial Rome, they keep their position only if they maintain their highest performance. Professional athletes are all contest; their "work" is constant proof of their right to be at the top. They are our present democratic equivalent of ancient and feudal nobility; they work at play and are accorded celebrity and wealth that staggers comprehension (Bok 1993).[2] Others who believe that they are stronger and quicker try to usurp their place. Those in contact sports are always in contest, facing powerful adversaries—the members of the opposing team—and their replacements if they fall behind. Football is advertised as battle. Success depends entirely on the coordinated and focused aggression of the team. Hard competitive sport and the viewing of it are close contenders for the equivalent of war, moral or not.

In 1993, David Williams, a Houston Oilers tackle, missed a crucial game against the New England Patriots to be with his wife during the birth of their baby. His wife had suffered a painful miscarriage the year before. The defensive coach of the Oilers, Bob Young, commented: "This is like World War II, when guys were going to war and something would come up but they had to go." He later added, "My [own] wife told me that she was going to have a baby and I said, 'Honey, I have to play a football game.' [But] David just went blank, he let the guys down; he let hundreds of thousands of fans down" (Verhovek 1993). Young's statement might seem off the mark to the uninitiated, but it is an accurate statement of what athletes and ardent fans believe to be at the center of hard sport.

Playing while hurt, staying in the fight despite desperate wounds, often assumes part of the male idea of war found in sport. By the time Mike Webster, a former center, was "enshrined" in the Pro Football Hall of Fame, the shock and concussion of the game had aged him beyond his forty-five years. He was also suffering from congestive heart failure, spasms, and convulsions. He spoke of his reduced physical condition to spectators and sportswriters at the ceremony. He found the metaphors of childhood: "All I have to do is finish the game . . . Like John Wayne said, 'I'll finish it, maybe not standing up, but I'll finish.'" He told the audience that they lose only if they "don't finish the game," and, if they finish, they win. His audience of sportswriters shouted his name, bellowing their love of him (Seabrook 1997).

Ardent fans, devoted to their team, become high at games, with and without drugs or drink. Men are swept away by the excitement of union with those who live at the sharp edge of contest. Some men are awed in the presence of professional athletes and seek closeness to them. The desire for identification can become literal. Men reach out to touch renowned athletes. Autographs and photographs are traded. Athletes' uniforms are highly valued, particularly those already worn on the field, with the lingering scent of the hero, detectable or imagined. Actor Dustin Hoffman recalled a prizefight in which an ecstatic fan, a male, pushed as closely as he could to the winning boxer, "wiping all he could of the sweat from the boxer's body onto himself" (Oates and Halpern 1988, p. 303).

Sports heroes become icons, and if they show indifference to their place in the communal male ethos, they are censured, in the way members of royal families are who let down the commoners. Athletes are criticized if they descend from the position of a champion athlete to mere entertainer: in his declining years, Joe Louis had to support himself as a greeter in a gambling casino. Athletes offer spectators identification with the hero of their fantasy and participation in the excitement of victory.[3] In exchange, spectators confer celebrity and wealth on athletes. If an athlete becomes a mere entertainer and abandons his past connection to the edge of unpredictable contest, he trivializes his exalted position. When he shows himself as ordinary and human, fans become angry over the loss of their part of the extraordinary, the fantasy of being one with the hero, *like* the hero, heroes themselves.

The lives of professional athletes, like ordained royalty, seem to encompass a larger reality than the commonplace activities of ordinary life. Their lives are imagined to be lived in constant clear focus, completely in the moment. The "real," for many (men), is found in the excitement of athletic contest, and paradise for men is sought in perpetual boyhood. Fans seek the fantasized merger with those men totally engaged in action with real physical risk.[4] Men are buoyed by such identification. War fantasies offer the same excitement, with even higher stakes, and a release from the routine of civilian life. Some boys seek that as soldiers.

SHAPING BOYS INTO SOLDIERS

Wars are fought by boys.

> —Paul Fussell, *Wartime: Understanding and Behavior in the Second World War*

I was a little boy made into a man.

> —George H. W. Bush (interview with Paula Zahn, *CNN Presents*)

Boys are usually seen as more physically aggressive than girls and groups of boys absolutely so. Conferring the privilege of aggression on a group of young males catalyzes and augments the innate chemistry for individual aggression.

War itself has been acclaimed as a celebration glorifying youthful action (Hynes 1991). Boys are readied for war in peacetime by predisposition and through social forces that use war as the distinguishing contest defining a man as different from a woman. In early rehearsal, boys play at war and joyfully mimic sudden contact with death. Small boys beginning their relationships with other boys become anxious about their untried strength, fearful of not measuring up. Toy stores sell a massive array of replica weapons, and only a few boys do not want them. Parents who value peace and oppose aggression often discover that withholding the toys does nothing to extinguish the intense desire for them. Parents usually capitulate to the supplications of their sons with misgiving, and they blame the manufacturers for seeking only gain in producing "real-looking" M-16s (Dyan 1997). Boys who are denied that type of toy use a hand or a stick to mimic a weapon.

Boys training to be soldiers remember when they played at war. In Vietnam, soldiers called the ammunition for their personal weapons "caps," after the harmless gunpowder noisemaker in the toy guns of their childhood. They say that they "capped" the enemy, that is, killed him, as they did as boys playing make-believe. Toy manufacturer Mattel even supplied the military with plastic stocks of the famously unreliable early model M-16A, and "MATTEL" was stamped in raised lettering on the plastic M-16 stocks.

A career of professional soldiering attracts boys with differing levels of athletic and leadership competence. Discipline, the promise of a rigorous life to which they are equal, and a place for their patriotic zeal attracts the best soldiers. In the mass of ordinary boys with ordinary ability at school or athletics, others seek a dreamed-of heroism or at least the realization of the promised manhood of recruiting posters. Boys have dreamed of war the way many girls dream of marriage. In the culture of the twenty-first century, however, girls also express aggression—in working life, relationships, sports, even war. As the politics of equality edges beyond levels of estrogen and testosterone, female soldiers take their place alongside male soldiers. Whatever the debate and discourse about comparative strength and habits, the tools of war are the great equalizers; anyone with determination, commitment, and the stomach for killing is eligible. It is doubtful though that the "brotherhood" of soldiering will actually transform into a "sisterhood."

War demands impetuousness and daring, a place for the attributes of boys, unlike primary school. At the beginning of the war with Japan, U.S. schoolchildren sang a popular song about "Johnny Zero." The lyrics describe a restless schoolboy unable to obey the rules. His one distinction: he repeatedly failed; each day he "got another zero." The song had a "hook," a turnaround, which children loved: Johnny goes to war for his country, is still called "Johnny Zero," but with new meaning. His past failures are exonerated; his impulsiveness and physical quickness continue to "get him zeros," that is, the Japanese aircraft the Zero. The war transformed him into the idolized Johnny Hero.

DIFFERING MORAL AND SOCIAL VIEWS OF WAR

> *Dulce et decorum est pro patria mori.* [Sweet and proper it is to die for your country.]
> —Horace, *The Odes of Horace*

> If you could hear, at every jolt, the blood
> Come gurgling from froth-corrupted lungs

obscene as cancer . . .

. . . you would not tell with such high zest

to children ardent for some desperate glory

The old lie: Dulce et decorum est.

—Wilfred Owen, *Dulce et Decorum Est*

The nation at war confers on the boy a reprieve from the ordinary; he is given the ultimate game to win, and because of war's high probability of death for the young who fight in it, he may not be required to grow old. The direction in which he must take aggression is now clear, the boundaries delineated by national purpose and military regulation, and within that the soldier is allowed, exhorted, commanded to take it to its limit. Training, weapons, and comrades all support the distancing from civilians. Peacetime mandates against aggression, disapproval by parents or other authorities, abstract threats of perdition or social banishment vaporize. Boys have been readied since childhood for such redirection of energy. War will make them men—at least, men as boys idealize them to be. Some boys volunteered for Vietnam certain of the moral necessity for the war meshed with achieving manhood.

As the war against Russia became desperate in 1945, a German soldier in deep privation and facing imminent death could write home, "Nothing can help us anymore . . . Prayers seem like vodka—they blunt the cold for a moment . . . I have been promoted to *obergefreiter* [corporal] . . . feel that much more important . . . [and now] I think these extraordinary and difficult moments have made us into men" (Sajer 1990, p. 402).

The Boy Scout movement began in England soon after the Boer War with the express purpose of improving the health of British boys through outdoor activity. The war against the Boers, in which victory was not as elegant and easy as first expected, supported the wish for developing strength to preserve the empire. The movement bore a military coloring from its beginning, and fitness for war was a large part of the theme. Baden-Powell's founding book, *Scouting for Boys*, exhorts the young reader to avoid the example of the last days of the Roman Empire, when "wishy-washy slackers . . . without patriotism" lost their empire. The motto of the Boy Scouts, "Be prepared," did not stand alone: "to die for your country . . . so that when the time comes you may charge home with confidence, not caring whether you are to be killed or not" (Bond 1986, p. 75).

Patriotism for the empire was resoundingly echoed in music and theater aimed at both youths and adults. The British implored the deity, "who made us mighty, make us mightier yet." Those stirring words of war for the British Empire in the Elgar processional have been drafted into service across the Atlantic and are still sung enthusiastically, anachronistically, unknowingly, and almost unfailingly at secondary school graduations in the United States. We are susceptible to the myths of contest and victory and borrow the most stirring from others and make them our own.

THE MOVIES

Adolescent boys try on the template created by the athlete, cowboy, and soldier icons. Movie images of heroes are powerful and enduring. The movies have celebrated the idea of physical dominance, the myth of the warrior, from its first flickering images. *The Great Train Robbery* was the first movie Western with a story line and narrative; central to the story is raiding and predation and the wide-open American West as opposed to the restrictions imposed by cities. Like *Genesis* and *The Iliad,* it is about force (Weil 1985; Niditch 1993). Such myths may effect decisions that lead to military action: President Nixon saw the movie *Patton,* looking for a sign to go ahead with the Cambodian incursion. At the time, he prayed for rain, imitating the general's action in the film (Gibson 1994). The boy in that president, continuing to play at war, summed the collected images of all past Saturday matinees to launch military actions with staggering mortal and political consequence. Buoyed by shared myths of boyhood, leaders direct, and boys follow the leader.

More than half of a group of Marine recruits at Camp Pendleton said that they joined the Marines because of the John Wayne movies they had seen. Often combatants see themselves in combat as in a movie, modeling themselves on that image of Wayne—the toughest guy in the world (Holmes 1989). Wayne emerged, as Garry Wills writes, as "the American Adam," full blown in the movie *Stagecoach.* Wayne entered our world from the movie screen as an armed man and became the personification of the American male ideal, a man of the frontier, mistrustful of book learning, cities, and foreign influence. He has solid, absolute certainty of what is right, and he "kills only that which needs killing." He carries with him no excess baggage, only the American "myth of the frontier" and the "mystique of the gun" (Wills 1997). Durable, he will finish the contest.

Through four wars, John Wayne shaped the ethos for boys as cowboys and soldiers, but men pulled into soldiering by images such as Wayne projected often feel duped after the horror of combat. A World War II soldier enjoyed seeing Wayne humiliated when he paid a surprise visit to wounded soldiers. "Somebody booed, then everybody was booing," and when Wayne tried to talk, the soldiers "drowned him out . . . Eventually he quit and left." Wayne was "the symbol of the fake machismo we had come to hate" (Morris [quoting William Manchester] 1996, p. 755).

Veterans who have survived "the test" of manhood become angry with those who simulate it and with movies that pushed them toward war's glories but did not help them when they got there. The war, for some, has underwritten a solid sense of self and has broken boyish myths. In peace, they can challenge the men who once had them in thrall—their fathers, the DI (drill instructor), John Wayne, even God. One former combatant told me that his friends pulled him out of a movie theater when he "lost it" and kept shouting at the screen, totally out of control, "Fuck you, John Wayne," in repeated sacrilege.

THE BOY BECOMES A SOLDIER

A quick, strong boy can be easily trained to take on a new persona by using ancient methods with newer techniques:

D.K.: You go in young, immature, they break you down and make you into a "fighting machine."

Dr.: Did you like it?

D.K.: No-o-o! In the beginning I was so scared, wanted my mother [laughs], but if it wasn't for the training, that S.O.B. DI, I wouldn't be here today [tearful, shakes head] . . . You go to fight and it was real, way beyond the real . . . You learned about life through death. You felt at bedrock, you were part of the earth, or something, yet . . . high . . . waiting for contact, and always so scared you couldn't imagine. Always hungry, thirsty, maybe in pain but, not noticing because I was in it, in it . . . I mean for the time you were there, as bad as it was . . . death and stink all around . . . you were in it—in life.

In the words of another Marine: "I was nothing before the Marines got me and I went to Vietnam. I became nothing again after that. The only thing that keeps my heart beating is my memories [of the war]" (E.P.).

Because he is set apart from his parents and family and trained for war, the soldier learns that his family has difficulty understanding him in his transformation. What they could demand from him in the past has no relevance to his new world, which is unevenly divided into military and civilian. There is pleasure in that earned independence from old restraints.

While only some men gladly accept mortal risk, most want to believe that at the instant they would be able to pass the test and not be dominated by fear. Boys are often propelled into risk and aggression against whatever judgment they could exercise because that is the way to be men. Recruits are informed that they are "pussies" until they pass the test of training and combat. Not all men passionately want to be heroes, but fewer can tolerate being called "coward." Most, if not all, boys worry about not being able to stand up to other boys in a "throw down," a real fight. Most boys have grown into men in our society knowing the necessity of standing up to other boys. Their place among their fellows often depends on taking that risk.

Boys are encouraged by their peers to battle against their mothers' instinct to comfort them. Their fathers, friends, and the DI—who is no friend—tells them that giving up the need for such comfort is essential to manhood and survival in the all-male environment of war. Mother also possesses the more awesome power of birth. More than one commentator has said that men at war approach the power women have, never quite achieving it. "[War] is, for men, at some terrible level the closest thing to what childbirth is for women: the initiation into the power of life and death" (Broyles 1984, p. 61).

MOTHERS

War is to men, as maternity is to women.

        —Benito Mussolini, in William Broyles's "Why Men Love War"

Male-dominated human societies, and that means nearly all societies, deprecate women. Some early psychoanalytic theorists locate the reason in men's awe of women's ability to produce life, the "maternal omnipotence" arising out of infant and child caretaking (de Beauvoir 1970). As men reach manhood—as part of it—young men in many Western societies act out their fear of dependency through a rejection of the feminine, of woman's power and control (Horney

1932).[5] Mother is desired and therefore also feared because she has produced life and exerts the strongest hold. Her presence promises total body comfort (Balint 1939).

A boy is shaped by his father and by society to struggle against his mother's power, to become strong and to stand as a man. Physical strength alone is unequal to that task; however, a boy has greater difficulty in struggling against the mother who made him, but training for war marshals a strong force against mother. Father urges his son to meet the conditions for manhood, and the DI is the clearest, explicit teacher of uncompromising aggressiveness and resilience.

Mother, who is the DI's enemy, is within her boy. The boy becoming a soldier is taught to fight against that which speaks of softness—his mother's voice inside him—under the threat of rejection as a soldier. His difficulty in the struggle against his mother is uncanny and does not come out of clearly appreciated reason or memory. His wish for her presence can stop him from achieving manhood. In training for war, he is forced to identify with the DI, the toughest man, a relationship with few doubts but much ambivalence. He fears and hates his DI, and the training and then the terror of combat forces the wish to be like him.

Boys are trained for combat by men who are usually more powerful and physically aggressive than the boys' fathers and who certainly have more proximal force to shape behavior and thought. Manhood is promised and given after hard contest, by the DI, by the Corps, supported through closeness and bonding with comrades. With that, the boy is separated from his dependent need for his mother, and there is less need for the blessing of his father as part of this rite of passage. The boy trades unformed youth for identification with his DI and his comrades.

The separation goes only so far, however. As recalled by one veteran, "After a firefight, you can hear wounded Marines calling for their mothers" (E.P.).

FATHERS

Women, it is true, create human beings, but only men can make men.

—Margaret Mead, *Male and Female*

Male sexual identity is relatively vulnerable; the certainty of manhood is easily shaken. Many men in our culture seek reinforcement of masculinity more compelling than rites of entry into manhood such as school and religious confirmations. Entry into manhood often means wearing the soldier's uniform. A father sees his son transformed by his uniform, looking lean and raw because of training, and says, "I guess that you are a man now." My father said that to me.

Fathers who are aware of their lack of heroism may see their own second chance in their soldier sons. The young soldier's uniform and weapons assert the investment of the power of the state in the boy, a power to which even his father is obedient. Facing danger in a shooting war, the son becomes the central family figure, its pivot and concern, the more meaningful to family cohesion.[6]

Sexual maturity and eligibility for marriage was once contingent on a male's proving himself by killing an enemy in battle (Marlow 1983). In groups of what anthropologists have termed *prestate peoples*, there still is a direct relationship between the ability to kill other men and reproductive success: the most aggressive warriors are said to take the greatest number of brides and have the most children (Chagnon 1983).[7]

Boys win manhood through trial and endurance. The common thread is that boys are not predetermined to become men, they must be made into men through contest managed by older men. Womanhood, in contrast, is deeded by biology and predestined in its arrival at menarche, rather than achieved by trial; it is often marked only by some commemorative ritual.

In Judges 8:1–20, Gideon captures the kings of Midian in battle. They admit that they had killed his brothers and are prepared for their own death. Gideon instructs his son, Jetha, to kill them. The text says that Jetha did not draw his sword, "for he feared because he was yet a youth." But it is not his father, Gideon, who encourages him to kill, but the captured kings; they accept their death as warriors and endorse its necessity. They exhort Jetha to rise and kill them. To be a man, Jetha must not flinch from killing, "for as a man is, so is his strength." Gideon must do what his son could not.

Older men in many societies make boys into men by tests of hardness, aggressiveness, and endurance of severe pain. Such rituals both solidify a beginning sense of manhood for the boy and provide instructions for the future, the continuing necessity to take "manly risks," to face mortal danger, in order to protect family and community. *Tewa* boys are whipped by their fathers who are dressed and masked as *Kachina* spirits and who proclaim to them afterward that "you are now . . . made a man" (Gilmore 1990).

The cost of failure is the enduring judgment that they are unformed, childlike (and effeminate). In many societies, men who do not match a cultural idea of what is masculine endure from both men and women a degraded status, with the threat that they will be made subordinate to a "real man," that is, viewed as a woman. That is reinforced first by their fathers. Hispanic men are prompted to subscribe to the idea of "machismo" in a nearly religious way; "real" men are termed *muy hombre,* and men can suffer enormous loss of status and self-worth if they are judged as *flojo* (empty, weak, useless, and impotent) for failing the standards of assertiveness with others. Their fathers fear a personal loss of status if they produce a son who is not *muy macho* (Gilmore 1990). On Truk, a boy is challenged with a mortal test for manhood: "Are you a man? [If not,] come I will take your life now" (Gilmore 1990, p. 12). Manhood, then, comes out of test.[8]

The tests include severe hazing, whipping, beating, scouring, bloodletting, scarring of skin among the Amhara of Ethiopia, the Masai of the Serengeti, Samburu of East Africa, the natives of New Guinea, and Native Americans. Among the Fox tribe of Iowa, boys must go through what their elders call "the Big Impossible," severe tests of competence in tribal matters and economic achievement.

Tests to become a man are not limited to prestate peoples or to those ethnic groups that continue arcane rituals. Some boys in the United States have sought their form of manhood out of contests of sexual daring. In 1993, a group of high school boys in Lakewood, New Jersey, calling themselves the "Spur Posse," coerced girls into having group sex and scored points toward respect from other boys by frequency of coitus (Hewitt et al. 1993).

Boarding schools for boys in England are known for a "trial by ordeal" that some adults who have been educated in these or similar schools justify as necessary to achieve the "social state of manhood." These "public schools" have historically reserved a place almost exclusively for upper-class boys, but now are open to others as well (Gilmore 1990).

Boys have the strongest wish to be accepted by their fathers, to be given manhood by their fathers, and at best to have the acknowledgment that it is possible to grow beyond them. They want their fathers to allow the struggle toward becoming their "own man," and that means some contest must take place. Some fathers will not really concede the competition with their sons. Father and son stay locked in a "zero-sum game," with father wagering his own manhood against his son's taking it. For the son, in modern Western societies at least, war promises the quickest and the riskiest possibility of grasping manhood, with and without Father's concession. Fathers lower the barrier for their sons who become soldiers, and fathers want to experience their sons' strength and glory and take a part of it as their own:

A Marine: "I'll tell you something, O'Brien. If I could have one wish, anything, I'd wish for my dad to write me a letter and say it's okay if I don't win any medals. That's all my old man can talk about, nothing else. How he can't wait to see my goddamn medals" (O'Brien 1990, p. 39).

One Marine who was severely wounded in Vietnam and suffering from the emotional aftermath speaks of his father's harshness toward him as he grew up, until he graduated from boot camp with honors: "My father came down to North Carolina all the way from Boston to see me graduate. When I came up to Boston on leave, he took me to his bar! He said to everybody, 'This is my son!' (his face glows). Never has been or will be anything like that. I don't care, I'd go through it all again for that feeling—father-son [weeps]" (D.K.).

Such a wish is not pure; there is usually anger mixed with yearning for the father's reluctant approval. When the soldier is distant from family, in the midst of training or combat, a father who is a problematic figure carries less influence and can be rejected. With decreased fear of punishment for violating societal laws or the commandments of God or God's lieutenants, one might even kill the father. Not all soldiers kill in war, and only the rarest will commit patricide, but the license and ability to kill energize such fantasies: "He was never for me. He never gave me any attention except to tell me I wasn't worth shit . . . What matters to me are my buddies. I don't need that son of a bitch for anything. Jesus, I always wanted him to like me, for something, for any reason, and he never gave it to me. Now he can go fuck himself. I'm free, and he can die" (O.I.).

HARD AGAINST SOFT

Love that which makes you hard.

That slogan was painted on the walls of a work camp for seven hundred Norwegian boys. They had been students and were captured after the invasion of their country and taken to Germany to convert them to the Nazi cause. That idea came from Himmler, who assumed that the tall, blond, and blue-eyed men who had been captured in the Norwegian resistance would soon volunteer to become SS soldiers. The prisoners were taken to "friendly" camps at first and exposed to continuous Nazi propaganda alternating with severe threats. None of the Norwegians volunteered to serve. As the war reversed for the Germans and the Norwegians showed no interest in conversion, they were moved to the "work camps" of Buchenwald and Neuengamme in 1944. One of the young men noted that "there it was written above the gate *'Jedem das seine'*—'Everyone gets what he deserves'" (Jarl Jorstad, personal communication).[9]

The Nazi ideal is a male culture of soldiers in constant battle with the rest of the world. That idea resides in many societies, where it meets more resistance than was found in the Third Reich. The exhortation, "Love that which makes you hard," on the walls of the "friendly" concentration camp is arresting and powerful because it has elements of complexity that take an interval to rise fully into awareness. The command is not just to endure privation, but for boys to embrace it as a lover; it conjoins male hardness and aggression with sex. It is a command to love only that which makes you hard. Male hardness is for penetration; it overcomes resistance; it demands rejection of what is soft or tender. What is rejected is the closeness with a woman that offers a man "total body tranquility," a sense of well-being after erotic striving that can reawaken the feelings of infancy, resembling a total sensory return to the mother's care (Balint 1939).

Such tranquility can blunt the soldier's hard edge. Sexual encounters for soldiers are accordingly typically presented as transitory. Some men back from Vietnam sadly acknowledge that war has taken their ability to be close to a woman; ironically, their tenderness is reserved only for their comrades in arms. Sex, like everything else, can become aggressive assault.

A returned Vietnam veteran says about making love: "She tells me, 'it's like bang, bang, bang, bang.' I feel it too—it's like I'm attacking her, not loving her. I don't know if I know how to do that. I just can't be that soft" (N.S.).

A German infantryman in World War II: "There was the war," Guy Sajer recalled, "and I married it because there was nothing else when I reached the age of falling in love" (Sajer 1990, Preface).

BOYS, FASCISM, AND THE IDEA OF WAR

War, the Father of all things, is also our father: it has hammered, hewn, and tempered us into what we are.

—Ernst Junger, *Storm of Steel*

Boys are malleable, and their society—their leaders and fathers—can shape the degree of adherence to the view that men are only hard and only soldiers. The Nazi movement entrained German boys toward military conquest and pulled them into attachment to the leader. German ideology made the hard warrior the primary symbol of the nation and German *Kultur* and war a celebration of boys in action proving German manhood. The leaders of the Third Reich most strongly delineated the place of boys in society and the standards of regard with which to judge them. The Nazis set out an extreme of Western attitudes for making boys into men. Yet Nazi leadership could not clearly articulate any coherent program or politics aside from romanticizing youthful energy and will; the Nazi idea elevated irrational social action to credo. Indeed, physical activity—motivated more by feeling than by thought—was emphasized to the exclusion of all else (Waite 1952; Theweleit 1987). Propaganda preparing for Nazi takeover attempted to sweep aside German rationality in an appeal to the elements of myth romanticizing war for youth that also resided in that nation. It proclaimed only action and command by leaders: "Leaders, leadership, that is our need; in obedience and great wordless activity . . . The new religion must be inarticulate . . . Convictions must be sealed in the dark . . . I want the fight and man naked and unashamed with sword in his hand; and behind, the stars sweeping westward and before the wind and the grass. It is enough, Brothers. Action! The word is spoken!" (Waite 1952, p. 19). The transition to manhood was decreed by the Nazis; soldiers were essential to the Third Reich, and boys would become men by making them soldiers.[10]

The Nazis held up before the Germans a mysterious story about the German past and a destiny presented as foreordained. The values of youthful activity directed toward conquest and subjugation of others destroyed a democratically organized state system in order to follow "the Fuehrer principle" (Waite 1952, pp. 19–21). The Fuehrer presented himself as unquestionable leader and the father to the unquestioning. The paradox bedeviling the Germans today is the contrast between their cherished civilized rationalism and their romantic ideas of the blood myth leading to war.

In contrast, boys in the United States and elsewhere in Western democracies are generally raised in an educational and political atmosphere of information exchange that promotes ambivalence toward leaders, who are not accorded anything resembling absolute power. That is the important pillar supporting democracy. But boys anywhere, and in any time, grow up with the understanding that older men control the social fulcrum of power and use it for their own ends. The elders possess the material wealth and the relationships with others like them that give them authority. Boys can feel overpowered by men in charge, pulled by a fierce desire to take the power that the old man has and a conflicting desire to be accepted, loved, and given manhood by him.

BOYS AND AGGRESSION

Human aggression in its social organizational sense is the propensity of males . . . The group will either split into competing coalition groups or seek external object for domination.

—Lionel Tiger, *Men in Groups*

The philosophers, psychologists, anthropologists, and biologists who see aggression as innate reason that we are catapulted from peaceful behavior not only by provocation but also because there is inside of us "the beast" constantly pressing to escape the restrictions of civilization. "Wars," Chagnon writes, in a study of the human group termed the most aggressive—the Yanomamo—"are rooted in the natural fierceness of the human male . . . If warfare and male sexism are 'natural' for all human societies, then there is no need to seek an explanation of warfare and male sexism in the specific [conditions for small populations of prestate peoples]" (Chagnon 1983, p. 213).

There are counters to that proposition, and in the case of the Yanomamo, specific social conditions do seem to matter. The Yanomamo restrict the number of girls and women (by neglect or female infanticide) and then fight over the fewer women. War in these circumstances is a culturally defined procedure rather than a runoff of innate male aggressive repertoires. The Yanomamo have shaped their culture toward war, and it is a socially required activity toward which all the boys

are trained. There can be little doubt that genetic factors set much of human behavior in motion, but such behavior does not run on rails. Culture and society
determine its manifestation as much as encryptment in DNA (Chagnon 1983).[11]

Culture and societal attitudes shape boys' aggression. In societies where boys
and girls are raised together, there is less violence than in those in which they are
segregated.[12] Social groups where men and women constantly share closeness
and child-care responsibilities are less violent than those that do not (Whiting
and Whiting 1975).[13] Although the absence of women in the rearing of boys may
not be linearly related to causes for the war in highly complex industrialized societies, there is some argument to be made for its being a secondary factor inciting war (Waite 1952).[14]

Many authors have addressed the reality of human aggressive drives as
counter to fairy tales; Freud, echoing Goethe, said that the story of human aggression is "not for children." But children also are quite capable of cruelty, by
indifference or by design. The playground is a difficult place for the weak, inept,
and unaggressive child. William Golding's coruscating novel *The Lord of the Flies*
(1954) underscores this fact to the extreme. Golding presents the brutish behavior of his boys as basic; the primitive environment simply wears off the thin
patina of civilization and innate savagery emerges. But we could also say with
equal force that the civilization evolved along with our genetic instructions and,
along with aggression, is part of our nature.

DYING YOUNG

All warlike people are a little idle and love danger better than travail.
    —Francis Bacon, "Of the True Greatness of Kingdoms and Estates"

In varying intensities, boys have an attachment to risk. For many boys, the
prospect of adulthood is drab, while war is exciting and exacting and offers a
prize for heroism that is worth a boy's risk. When a boy dies as a soldier, he becomes a man at that moment.

Not all young men give themselves easily or instinctually to death, but men
in combat will give up their lives in self-sacrifice for comrades or in obedience to
leadership, not invariably, but often enough and memorably.

The U.S. Nisei Battalion flag declared "Go for broke," meaning "bet it all," that is, put your life down in this one moment—win or die. Such recklessness is an affirmation of the vitality in a boy's life, shared and possibly to be lost with and for the closest friends. There is in that, also, a semblance of nobility and immortality. There is, in that, the attraction of war for boys.

As the most intense part of the game of life, "rough sport in the open air," war demands that boys give up their youth with its impetuosity. A British poem of World War I exhorts the schoolboy-now-soldier to do as he did on the athletic field, to "play up, play up, play the game." At the battle of the Somme, it was reported that Captain Nevill started to lead his Eighth East Surreys forward by kicking a football toward the German machine guns when a bullet found him (Ferguson 1998).

Real enthusiasm for combat is felt by uninitiated youthful troops (Dunnigan 1988). They are strong and resilient and, given an iron doctrine, most will obey command. Above all, at first, they are "innocent about their own mortality" (Keegan 1976). "On the plane going over to 'Nam, we were pumped, tough, grabbing the bar over our heads and doing chin ups—like electricity in all of us, unbeatable, nonstop. Had to have the war, had to have the war" (E.P.).

The *Hagakure*, a sixteenth-century Japanese Bushido text explaining the "Way of the Warrior," affirms the idea that "the way of the warrior is death" (Harries and Harries 1991). Soldiers inducted into the Japanese Imperial Army were measured simultaneously for uniforms and for coffins. The Prussian Army instructed recruits in *Kadaverdisziplin*, obedience to duty until death (Waite 1952). German soldiers of the Third Reich marched into a training camp under a banner that declared, "We Are Born to Die" (Sajer 1990).

The idea of self-sacrifice was not an exclusively German or Japanese creation, however. Before and during World War I, English commanders believed that the outcome would be decided by the moral qualities of self-sacrifice residing in individual British soldiers. They disdained technical advances in weaponry, particularly ordnance. Ethical philosophers of war believed that "victory would go to the army that had been trained to die rather than to avoid dying" (Bond 1986, p. 93). Winston Churchill, who had earlier strongly supported the costly and doomed campaign in Gallipoli, rued the arrogant stupidity of the commanders in World War I who "engaged machine gun bullets with the breasts of brave young men" (Churchill 1982, p. 4). This cadaver morality was supported by the relatively higher numbers of British as opposed to German fatalities, despite the Entente's greater availability of weapons (Fergueson 1998).

There is little doubt among military commanders that the soldier who has the willingness to die and is not preoccupied with living, more than with doing his task of killing, is the best soldier. One historian of the U.S. armed forces put it, "final, full acceptance that his name is already written down in the rolls of the already dead [to do his duty] . . . under fire" (Harries and Harries 1991).

That realization forced itself on many young infantrymen. The German *Landser* (soldier) in World War II often fought with the certainty of death: "Then we would fire in a lunatic frenzy without mercy. We didn't wish to die and would kill and massacre as if to avenge ourselves in advance . . . with fury, because we hadn't been able to exact enough retribution" (Sajer quoted in Fritz 1995, p. 68). Every *Landser* eventually came to understand that survival on the battlefield depended mostly on mysteries of fate or accident; combat is "not a romantic adventure" but a continual series of shattering incidents, until many decided that "only an ambulance or a grave digger offered a way out" (Fritz 1995, p. 68). The soldier's ability and behavior had only the smallest role.

For many of the boys who fought in Vietnam, combat lifted a corner of the expected universe. They experienced a world in war moved only by uncompromising necessities, where life and death were regulated by immediacy (or accident), stripped of the rules and conventions. Some boys achieved a precocious manhood, conferred on them by the intensity of the experience, the power of their brotherhood and weapons. Many felt strong, exultant, and empowered after survival in Vietnam in the fellowship of their comrades; on return, they felt dysphoria, anomie. Peacetime could give them no equivalent and demanded compliance to rules they had abrogated to survive. Their feelings are echoed by those of other soldiers in different places and times: "And if we survived, it was as madmen, never able to readapt to the peacetime world" (Fritz 1995, p. 68).

Boys went to Vietnam for all kinds of reasons, among them to pass the test of manhood. Many returned from Vietnam prematurely and harshly aged by the experience. It was difficult afterward for them to admit that their country had lost the war, and too many have discovered that they lost any chance for personal peace.

LeRoy G. Schulz
Emeritus Professor
West Virginia University
Morgantown, WV 26506

CHAPTER **TWO**

BROTHERS AND COMRADES

[Comradeship] does not demand for its sustenance the reciprocity, the pledges of affection, the endless reassurances required by the love of men and women. It is, unlike marriage, a bond that cannot be broken by a word, by boredom, or by anything other than death.

—Phillip Caputo, *A Rumor of War*

The reality of killing or being killed is muted through comradeship. Even death does not break the connection. There is a strong wish to reunite with past brothers, including those now dead. Lost friends continue to inhabit the lives of those who survive:

When the family does something [demeaning] to me, I leave and go to my room. I'm trying not to argue with my family—so I talk to Connors and Singleton and they talk back, we talk shit, we talk about what we did, like heating soup while fins [mortar fire] are incoming. Like the time we said to the FNGs [new recruits] that the VC had choppers . . . or the VC chased us in tanks. The guys said, scared, 'Tanks?' We had them going. We were always doing that, worrying each other . . . like, 'Watch it [to the] right—VC.' Like we knew it couldn't get worse so we made it sound as if now something worse could happen, and that was a joke. Well, it relieved us, like we could take even worse than worst . . . The closeness, you can't imagine anything like it. My people would do anything for me, risk their lives to get you water if you needed water. I'm not crazy but, God, there is nothing like that here, that is, back in this world, back in so-called civilization. That's why there is nothing left for me. (E.P.)

Some veterans have difficulty finding the right word to describe friends who are more than friends. *Buddy* seems too much a peacetime commonplace. *Tight buddy* indicates that there is a bond exceeding the usual and is reserved for the "brother" for whom you would indeed lay down your life. To a veteran, this "tightness" with soldiers he absolutely trusts is as strong as blood relationships or stronger, deeper and somehow more ancient. The term *comrade* is used throughout the world to refer to a military companion. *Comrade*, derived from the Latin word for chamber (*camera*), conveys a depth of attachment beyond what is ordinary and expected in peacetime. It came to mean a soldier with whom one shared the barracks room or tent, but it is foreign in sound and not used by U.S. veterans of Vietnam, who prefer the term *brother*. Combat brotherhood is like erotic love, intoxicating in mergers of youthful strength. Among soldiers who become comrades, there is a reshaping of self that blurs the boundaries between each of the members of the platoon, so that "'I' passes insensibly into a 'we,' 'my' becomes 'our,' and individual fate loses its central importance" (Gray 1970, p. 90). It makes men feel so alive that, in one more of the paradoxes of war, they often can accept death easily.

DEINDIVIDUATION, BONDING, AND AGGRESSION

Submergence of self for the good of the group eases the acceptance of death. The process of stripping individuals of familial values to ensure a uniform group response bears the cumbersome designation *deindividuation*. It occurs regularly in any group, even without the conscious guidance of leaders, in greater or lesser degrees and for varying periods of time. "Prosocial behaviors," affiliativeness, and religious experiences often occur as a part of deindividuation (Diener 1980). An uplifting experience of deeply felt and shared community may occur (Morris 1996). The exclusivity of intense affection for the group does not, however, always produce a moral, ethical, and just cause. Deindividuation can also result in the most horrendous episodes of human violence: the behavior of groups of schoolboys escalates as the group bends and breaks individual constraints on aggression. The boy merges with the group, achieves protective anonymity, and loses his sense of individual responsibility. That shift often creates a startling change in values and behavior (Festinger, Pepitone, and Newcomb 1952).[1]

Deindividuation creates its own morality; and it can be the exclusive love for the defined group and little for the rest of humanity. A group may be tightly disciplined like an army or it can be an anarchic mob. It usually includes aggression directed toward those defined as alien. Bill Buford, an American editor and writer, described his journey with "the thugs," English football hooligans. The fans were feverishly "pumped" and drunk before, during, and after football matches. They deliriously destroyed property and seriously injured supporters of the opposite team. The electric feeling that came with being caught up in the turmoil of the mob seemed bizarre only on reflection. Buford became strangely seduced by the thugs' company; he was caught in "a druggy high . . . in a state of adrenaline euphoria . . . What was it like for me? An experience of absolute completeness" (Buford 1993, p. 205).

People of all nations are susceptible to this group force, some more demonstrably than others. When a nation and its leaders support an attack against enemies, the nation can become as one in massively released aggression. People rally to despots. When Hitler declared his intention to destroy all that was alien to the state, crowds in Nuremberg answered with one assenting voice (Goldhagen 1997).

People embrace group attitudes and reject previously held individual values in many contexts, in nations, in organizations, and in mobs. It is the nightmare presented by Orwell in his prediction about the world of *1984*. Marine combat training forges an iron identification with comrades and the Corps. Training is designed to pull recruits forever from their past, instilling in them a new self-definition. They must now view themselves as Marines—hypermale—rejecting of all that is civilian and soft.

One former U.S. Marine clearly recalls the intensity, if not the exact words, of full-bore instruction for obedience, fired at his group by his DI (drill instructor), which all recruits in all services have heard with slight variations during basic training everywhere: "You're pussy. Forget your mother / father / sister / aunts / uncles—your family. I am your family . . . Don't look to anyone else for help— I'm God. Either I will make you into a man, a Marine, a fighting machine, or you'll die trying" (N.P.).

In the frantic pace of early Marine Corps training, the cadre places continuous pressure on the recruits to perform in an alien environment, to renounce all that is civilian and soft. At the start of boot training at Parris Island, South Carolina, constantly shouted commands keep the recruits moving. They are documented and inoculated, pushed in groups to exhaustion, harried toward the singleness of group response. After that, they are ready to have the Marine identity impressed on them (Morris 1996). When that happens, it is as if they have been seeking it all of their young lives. They learn to call each other "brother," and when they greet each other with "*Semper Fi*" even long after discharge from service, they are marking loyalty to their brothers and allegiance forged out of ferocious ambivalence toward *the Corps* (Shatan 1977).

Allegiance is forced on the unit or corps. The DI demands that personal loyalties not compete with loyalty to the Corps. Love of women (aside from sexual desire) is markedly decreased, and women are kept at a distance because the soldier must separate from any softness within himself. Friendships that come up against Corps discipline also meet with strong opposition. One former Marine was once in the training pool at Parris Island and believed that his closest friend was drowning; the DI beat him over the head to unconsciousness with a long pole to stop his rescue attempt (R.O.).

Although Marines have fantasies about killing the DI, they learn that training must equal the uncompromising cruelty of combat. The DI knows of their savage dreams of murder and realizes that he is doing a good job. Those who survive the training do not want it changed; by surviving it, they proved themselves equal to it. They won against the DI, who would reluctantly acknowledge their manhood. It becomes their most precious prize. They believe that other soldiers in other, softer services achieve such manhood cheaply and have no hold on authenticity (Shatan 1977).[2]

Similarly, those who survive U.S. Army Special Forces training to become Green Berets are pushed beyond normal limits of resilience. Driven in long, rapid marches without provisions, they live on vegetation and kill swamp animals, rats, frogs, and insects for food. Their relationship annealed in extremes of adversity gives them the solid comradeship with other men who also hold the honorable identity of the warrior. They are bound by shared hardships endured and by their shared ability to survive in the fiercest combat (D. Grossman, personal communication).

In an insensate passing, individual civilian values are replaced by those of the group. Increased aggressiveness is fostered and implemented by training. Commanders are officially required to levy severe punishment on soldiers' use of force outside of the rules. However, local command is often quite indulgent of soldiers' aggression against others outside of their group, such as other platoons or civilians or members of other branches of the military, as long as civilian authority does not step in because of public outcry. The strength of the group grows with collision. Such fights affirm collective new manhood and the exclusive solidity of the bond with the group.

A final letter home from a soldier who died in Iraq defines the bond: "Life here continues to be challenging, but we're all hanging in there . . . I still love being a commander. I love leading troops and taking care of them. It is a huge responsibility and I feel the weight of it everyday. I send the thing I love most out here—my men—into harm's way everyday and every night. I just do my best to ensure they're ready, trained, equipped and properly led in every situation" (Byers 2003).

The men in the group love each other for their shared loyalty. Out of the security of belonging to the group and to the Corps, these men can grow into a new self-confidence. In the nineteenth century, LeBon first formally described shared loyalty as a psychological phenomenon, but in an army, replacing old, individual family loyalties with new ones reaches back into human history. The oath of the ancient Chinese military order Hung League (A.D. 185) states: "I shall know . . . neither father . . . mother . . . , but the brotherhood, there shall I follow. . . . Its foe shall be my foe" (Tiger 1969, p. 135).

A similar shift in allegiance is found in a gentler context, but with the same hard resolve, in the New Testament: when Christ is told that his family is outside the meeting place with his disciples, he responds: "Who is my mother . . . and who are my brethren?" He gestures to his disciples and says, "Behold my mother and my brethren" (Matthew 12:47–49; Mark 3:31–34).

Those who train men for combat know that deindividuation shifts men toward sacrifice for the group. Close-order drill was used by the Sumerians in the third millennium B.C.E. for inculcating the group response and obliterating the individual will of the ground soldier (McNeill 1982). Drill and march have always been a part of military training. The Egyptian armies in close order stepped off "by the left," just as in every army since; the Roman army assembled in prescribed ranks and rows (Dyer 1985). In the seventeenth century, drill had become a part of the daily work of troops. Instituted by Louis XIV's secretary of state for war through his assistant, Lieutenant Colonel Martinet, the latter's name endures as a term for any commander who adheres to the details of hard discipline (Mc-

Neill 1982). Despite its irrelevance to present combat, parade drill close-order march is seen as essential to training, solidifying the group's single purpose and tying the morale and morals of the soldier to the group ethos. Morals and morale are entwined in the soldier. The shared, sacred oath of allegiance to cause and to comrades raises the spirits of all, giving them strength for battle (Geyl 1986).

FIDELITY

> Men are true comrades only when each is ready to give up his life for the other, without reflection and without thought of personal loss.
>
> —J. Glenn Gray, *The Warriors: Reflections on Men in Battle*

In war, relationships with trusted friends are more than friendships. Men give up their lives for comrades, a sacrifice that defies the strongest biological imperative for self-preservation and in that defines a form of nobility (Kojeve 1991).

Such acts present bewildering antinomies; love is apart from and yet a part of war. In combat, the closeness of bonding says more good about men than their actions speak of the bad. Friendship forged in combat was, for some combatants, the "one decent thing we found in a conflict otherwise notable for its monstrosities" (Caputo 1977, p. xvii). Streams of Vietnam veterans regularly, if reluctantly, visit the Vietnam Memorial, where, partly obscured from passersby, they cry softly and fear an "emotional breakdown" (the soldier's worst fear). In this place of homage to fallen friends with its numbing registration of abundant death, tokens of affection—letters, beer, cigarettes, medals, photographs, even an occasional lipstick—are left as visitors touch the names of the loved and departed.

Such feelings fade only slightly after the war. A soldier of World War II said: "We loved war for many reasons, not all of them good. The best reason we loved war is also its most enduring memory—comradeship" (Broyles 1984, pp. 56, 58).

War's romance contains the same elements as love (James 1911). Combatants describe, amid chronic fear of death, an acceptance of its probability and the unambiguous fidelity with other men. Soldiers love each other, with the sexual implications of such attachment usually elided.

Only some combat veterans embrace all other veterans as "brother," echoing Henry at Agincourt:

We few, we happy few, we band of brothers;

For he today that shall shed his blood with me,

Shall be my brother; be he ne'er so vile,

The day shall gentle his condition.

—William Shakespeare, *Henry V,* act 4, scene 3, lines 60–63

Even with the softening that time imposes on memory, combat soldiers do not generously extend themselves to any veteran of that era. They are wary of all those who call themselves "combat veterans" and are alert to catch them in a lie by asking detailed questions. The rage at the enemy who tried to kill them and who killed their comrades is accompanied by contempt for those who never saw battle or never knew the love for their comrades that comes with it; they reserve their greatest contempt and murderous rage for those who falsify or magnify their combat experience. Comrades close and known are still referred to as "my people." A Marine Corps sergeant who had served in Vietnam says, "I knew my people . . . After I was in-country for a while, I only had worries about my people, taking good care of them, we would do anything for each other. My people, not [laughs derisively] the whole so-called Armed Forces. The Army? We called them 'nonessential personnel.' But my people, they would give up their life for you, just do it, not a word, not a whimper" (R.O.).

In the trenches of World War I, the chief "prop" to morale *mates.* Their sharing and being in it together diffused anxieties and placed those feelings outside of the individual self. Lord Moran wrote of the way men coped with fear: "There is no answer to fear. It shakes the foundations of the mind. Physical contact [with comrades] is the only thing that helps" (Winter 1979, p. 137). In Vietnam, a soldier was limited to the perimeter occupied by himself and his friends, "my guys," the ones with whom he felt safe. Friends diminish combat's constant terror; a soldier without loyal brothers has a decreased probability of survival.

A former German soldier who faced what seemed like certain death in a Russian winter wrote of volunteering for an infantry combat unit: "This decision almost cost us our lives many times, but even now, looking back on everything that happened, I cannot regret having belonged to a combat unit. We discovered a sense of comradeship which I have never found again, inexplicable and steady, through thick and thin. . . . We smoked and joked over nothing—a 'nothing' that in fact represented the most absolute human joy I had ever known" (Sajer 1990, p. 13).

Loyalty to commanding officers does not always mirror the affection soldiers have for each other. A green soldier struggles to maintain the myth of his individual importance to the leader. In war, that idealization of the relationship between a commander and his troops often fades over time, unless the officer is extraordinary. The soldier will be most loyal to the competent commander who is close to him, leading his company or platoon on the line.

The common soldier who survives war sometimes figures out his place in it. Twenty-five years after he left Vietnam, one veteran clearly recalled: "We don't count. It was all fixed . . . They could do whatever they wanted to us. We went—there is always someone who will 'go.' That's us, the ordinary kids, ha—the boys. One of us goes [and] the others, the friends, go . . .We loved each other for it and still do, I'm not afraid to say it . . . and we would still go, we would go again, we *will* go again, because that is the way or *what* we are. We still believe, have to believe, it was right to go and do what we did" (E.P.).

They blame that part of their command that was uncomprehending of their suffering and indifferent about the deaths of their brothers. They often recognize the gulf between those in charge of the war and themselves as pawns: "We count for nothing. They use us to keep things good for themselves. We don't have a part in it. But we go to war as if we were fighting and dying for something for ourselves, for us—but it is for them—those at the top. It's all a matter of class or rank. We are easily fooled because we want them to accept us, to give us something of what they have lots of. They won't do it—they leave us nothing" (R.M.).

After surviving combat, soldiers may immediately feel relief, strength, and mastery; when they share these feelings with friends, there is a discovery of communal joy in the dark heart of war. The exaltation of combat transports men outside of themselves to merge with their comrades. "Liberated from individual impotence" and self-regard, they achieve a personal sense of immortality (Gray 1970). This degree of loyalty between comrades is expected in war and exceeds the trust felt with wife or family. A spouse is sometimes perplexed by its continued importance: "You know what I said to my wife when she asked me what it was I got out of the reunion with my buddies from the 'Cowboys' [helicopter fighter group in Vietnam]? I told my wife that the center of the feeling I have at the reunion is safety. I never feel as safe as when I'm with them . . . She kind of understands it, but I wouldn't expect her to *know* it" (G. Offringa, personal communication).

At a convention of World War II bomber crews fifty years after that war had ended, the same feelings were still present, evergreen for men into their ninth decade (Joseph Sonnenreich, personal communication). Amid the terror of combat, feelings of group loyalty and disregard for self coexist. Men pray for war's end; some wish for their own death to end combat's terror. Life is not worth much when it can be taken away so easily and capriciously. However, as grunts become "short-timers," about to be rotated "out of country," the value of their lives increases, and they become less likely to take the same risks because they can see a future. As the time neared to leave Vietnam, many veterans seriously considered extending their tours. On impulse and against reason, some remained with their buddies. Just as often, their comrades would angrily object and urge them to leave rather than gamble on a thinned-out chance for survival. Their closeness to one another was worth the sacrifice of their lives, but the war was unworthy of it.

Short-time soldiers who extended their tours did so because if they left their comrades, they would feel an irreparable sense of loss, like a death. That love of brothers was so intense that they knew, even in-country, that there could be no peacetime replacement (G. Offringa, personal communication).

During the "Hundred Hour War" against Iraq, many former Vietnam combatants wanted, often desperately, to go to the Gulf. That desire, as they know, yet also deny, bends and breaks the rational. They shared fantasies about how they could manage it, not so much to be in combat, but to help the young soldiers: "I just want to teach them how to stay alive . . . I really wanted to go—even had figured out how to get on a military transport . . . I could tell them how to do it, throw away the book . . . I know how" (V.E.). These older men, many at their half-century, wanted to return to the excitement of battle, to reconnect with their youth. They wanted to be father and brother to the young combatants.

COMRADES, VIOLENCE, AND REQUISITE COURAGE

They carried their reputations. They carried the soldier's greatest fear, which was the fear of blushing. Men killed and died, because they were embarrassed not to . . . It was what had brought them to the war in the first place, nothing positive, no dreams of glory or honor, just to avoid the blush of dishonor. They died so as not to die of embarrassment.

—Tim O'Brien, *The Things They Carried*

At the start of military training, the weak—physically maladroit, easily distracted, or slow to obey commands—are recognized, demeaned, and set aside into a "fuck-up platoon." Such a soldier is important in training to contrast with the desirable man, the alert, physically able, and mentally tough man, who you want as a buddy and friend—a brother—who can go with you to and through the fire.

Killing the enemy strengthens bonds. Combat pressures soldiers to obey the imperatives of group survival—to soldier—and to be one with their comrades. That demands, at that instant, a negation of lifelong attitudes. To not comply in combat, to think and behave as an individual rather than as a member of the group, to not kill with the others, even if it is "bad" killing, means the loss of love and the terror of isolation. Soldiers who are disloyal to the group fail the test and are deemed unworthy to be with other men. There is little that is conditional about it, and there is no regard for individual moral sentiment. Killing in the lopsided rationality of combat can also be done for love (O'Brien 1994).

When men engaged in atrocity, those who were unable to share in the group aggression were hated by other members of the group and attacked. A veteran, who was eighteen years old in Vietnam, says at first he could not go along with the acts of his fellow soldiers: "We drove by a field, some farmer working with his wife, maybe kids . . . They would shoot the buffalo, shoot him, the wife. I was on the twin 50s [.50-caliber machine guns]. I couldn't do it at first, then I had to because the guys wouldn't be with me, help me. I was alone, they would have pushed me out, I would have been alone. So I fired the guns, but not at anybody . . . Maybe I killed someone, I don't know. Then I killed with them, sometimes just because they wanted me to. I'm not like that, I'm not like that, honest. If my sergeant hadn't taken care of me I would be dead" (A.D.).

In groups, soldiers coerce compliance. To resist alone is difficult; compliance is necessary to not splinter the group. Combat groups are psychologically organized around male power, with the ability to use uncompromising force as the marker for manhood and worth. The soldiers who resist coercion toward illegal action in war, following their own values and the rules of war, must have extraordinary inner strength. They can lose comradeship, they can be called "coward," and their death becomes more probable.

The soldier's loyalty to comrades is assumed and used by command. The German infantry continued to fight in World War II long after it was clear that the war was lost and that their leaders had brought them to catastrophe.

Willi Heinrich wrote about German infantry on the Russian Front: "Our men [the *landsers*] no longer have any ideals . . . They're fighting for nothing but their naked lives, for their bedeviled unfortunate flesh . . . It can be used; it can be abused. And it has suffered abuse because it has been lured by the bait of so-called ideals. It has been killed and it has been allowed to kill, until it seems to exist only for its own sake. But behind all that there is the common soldier's fundamental decency which doesn't permit him to leave his comrades in the lurch" (Heinrich 1956, p. 138).

But the decency of the common soldier is too easily taken up by loyalty and yoked to corrupt principles or foundered purpose. The soldiers, aged by war, are fighting for their lives and fighting for each other, but their comradeship—undeniable, human, and altruistic—can be used for a corrupt purpose or for a corrupt leader and is, itself, corrupted.

THE COWARD

Come on, you sons of bitches. Do you want to live forever?
—Gunnery Sgt. Dan Daly, U.S. Marine Corps, Belleus Wood, June 6, 1918

He which hath no stomach to this fight,
Let him depart; his passport shall be made,
And crowns for convoy put in his purse;
We would not die in that man's company
That fears his fellowship to die with us.

—William Shakespeare, *Henry V*

One Vietnam veteran officer, a distinguished Marine platoon leader and author, characterizing the soldiers who failed, takes a relativistic view (unusual for combatants) that those who cannot learn to kill effectively may be good men in other situations: "It's extremely complex but as the officer lieutenant, I recognized that I had to balance my people [with regard to ability] . . . There is a category of people who just didn't belong there. I wouldn't call them cowards—they didn't belong, they couldn't do it, they couldn't deal with it and so you did everything you could to get them out quickly and honorably. So I'm not saying this in a derogatory manner. A coward is dangerous to everybody else so you didn't like him, but the job wasn't likable either, so not liking doing this at all is something you accept" (Fred Downs, personal communication).

But bonding in combat is intense and exclusive, and there is little room for anyone outside of the circle of comrades: "No, whenever I see someone I think, how would he do with me in 'Nam? Some guys just don't make it, they hide, even some Marines" (E.P.). The man who is not given to taking risks can be tolerated if not liked by comrades so long as he does not demonstrate absolute disregard for his fellows in self-saving cowardice. But the combatant who, in a decisive moment, refuses to soldier, who refuses to expose himself, to return fire, or hold his position is severely judged and often punished by his fellows if not his command.

The coward is abandoned or isolated and that often results in his death. It is expected among seasoned combatants that some will take greater risks than others. It is also expected that the grim necessity of their business will move even the most tentative to rise to an instant demand and not hang back, to take necessary personal risks for their fellows. Failing to do that endangers them all. Soldiers feel that a man found to be a coward should be killed because of the danger he imposes on others.

The coward revealed in war shows love only for himself and has not learned to accept death: "The coward's inner poverty of life and love make him no fit antagonist . . . The coward, unrelated to his fellows, has an insufficient hold on life and is not in charge of himself or his fate . . . But for the coward death is within him . . . The more he struggles to escape the greater is his captivity. When the coward's body is finally yielded up to death, there is nothing instructive or solemn about the spectacle. Few scenes are more deeply unpleasant" (Gray 1970, pp. 115–16).

THE ENEMY AS FRIEND

Killing is not without its regrets. Sometimes there is a merger, perhaps more true for the victor, with the killed and conquered enemy more than there is with dead comrades. Soldiers have taken the names of those conquered and killed. This was a tradition in the Roman Empire as in the case of the Roman general Scipio Africanus.

Genghis Khan's birth name, Temu-jin, was taken from a tribe his father had annihilated. Among Native Americans, the scalp of a killed enemy was brought back to the warrior's house and handled reverently. The victor communed with the man he had killed and the scalp told him how to be a great warrior. The dead warrior spoke to him as a father, an instructor whom he has conquered (Ehrenreich 1997).

The enemy who fought bravely, the one you wanted to destroy, is often immortalized in your stories, the deadly encounter perpetuated in memory, the victor alive and sentient. The brave fighter gains his opponent's respect when the battle is over.

The warrior reflects on the battle best won against a worthy opponent. They have had the common experience of combat. After the conflict is over, the enemy can be celebrated, treated as worthy of respect, almost, if not exactly, a comrade. Retired General Westmoreland visited Vietnam and embraced his old adversary, General Vo Nguyen Gap, who commanded the army of North Vietnam. They were, in the logic of war, brothers.

The ordinary kids belong to what the noble Henry embraced at the start of the terrible battle as "a band of brothers," all comrades together, as he spurred his troops on to battle on St. Crispin's Day at Agincourt (*Henry V*, act 4, scene 3). At the very end of Shakespeare's play, however, with the sweet, hard-won victory in his grasp, the noble Henry asks for an accounting of the dead, of the French, then of the English. But then there is a return to the primacy of lineage and he discounts the soldier, "not of name" as not a brother. The following statement from the herald ends the play:

Where is the number of our English dead?
[herald gives another paper]
. . . Edward the Duke of York, the Earl of Suffolk, Sir Richard Kikely, Davy Gam, Esquire,
None else of name.

PART II
KILLING AND KILLERS

THREE

KILLING
GETTING THE JOB DONE

A deep calm drenches the male soul when it feels the persona it inhabits being firmly screwed into a socket in some iron hierarchy or other, best of all a hierarchy legitimately about killing.

—Norman Rush, *Mating*

War . . . permits . . . conflict by armed force. It is also . . . a moral condition, involving the same permissiveness, . . . at the level of armies and individual soldiers. Without the equal right to kill, war, as a rule-governed activity would disappear . . . The soldiers who fought in [*Korea*] were moral equals even if the states were not.

—M. Walzer, *Just and Unjust Wars*

No matter how the business of war is adorned by parades, uniforms, and literary glorification of the warrior's courage, and however it is burdened by administration and logistics, the soldier's real work is in killing. The soldier's privilege to kill is unlike anything most other individuals have ever experienced, and the soldier who kills is permanently changed, fixed to the death he has made.

Years after, veterans still find memories of combat victory and killing exhilarating. Soldiers as yet "uncooked" by combat often scrutinize the face and body of the killed enemy in wonder at their ability to create something as profound and enduring as death. Soldiers tie themselves to the dead by photographing dead enemy soldiers or by taking the possessions of the dead as trophies to preserve the moment.

The terror of the first confrontation with enemy soldiers bent on killing sparks a feeling never felt before, and the victory after mortal contest creates a moment crystallized in time, distinct among other memories—a reference point for a life.

BLOOD SPORT, SACRAMENT, MYSTERY

Hunting and blood sport share some of the exhilaration soldiers find in war. Blood sport has the finality imposed by death—the victor and the vanquished, a circle closed.

Although the prohibition on killing is the sixth of the Ten Commandments, it is the strongest and most clearly defined sacred limit on individual action. Secular societies allow killing only conditionally, within boundaries defined by mitigating circumstances.

Another life can be permissibly taken for food, within broad limits. The ritual slaughter of specified animals, for food and symbolic reasons, ties the spilling of blood to God as well as to human need. The way in which animals are killed and become food is a part of many religious observances. The spilling of blood taints the slayer in the eyes of society—unless the act of killing is within regulations and the killer is given the privilege to kill by the state or by religious authorities. Laws, regulations, and commandments can transform the killing of all animals, including humans, into a sacrament. The secular state sanctions only some killing and also rigidly defines who or what, when, where, and with which means. The state maintains a monopoly on the use of force.

Those opposed to blood sports suggest "hunting" with a camera—an equal exercise of skill, patience, and physical prowess—a "moral equivalent" of blood sport. Why is it necessary, the proponents of the photographic hunt ask, for the hunt to end in a kill? Because photographing the quarry is not drama, it lacks death's profundity. Although they know that killing is their essential purpose, good hunters have the option of deciding not to kill even after an intense chase. With the quarry in his sights, the hunter does not fire if he feels uncertainty about being able to make a "clean kill." The skilled hunter has contempt for the "butcher," for whom any kill by any means suffices. The good hunter believes that hunting is for the few, for those proficient in skills learned over time. Some see it as participation in a mystery, a reunion with our distant past as predators (Kerasote 1993).

Care and respect for the animals whose blood is shed lift the hunter above the ordinary. Blood is a sacrament, and only the worthy should hunt. By care, skill, risk, and recognition of the relationship to the hunted, the hunter comes out of the kill ennobled by supremacy over the animal whose life he has taken. He could not have that experience without death; his dead quarry has given him a gift. Hunters often express affection for the killed quarry, for allowing the assertion of the hunter's ascendancy, for proving again the dominance of the hunter over the hunted. The hunter also gains an assertion of ownership of place; he has reintroduced himself into his own history, revisited the landscape of his primitive past, and again triumphed in it. There is an esthetic in such exercise of dominance; the hunter who has made a clean kill or tracked a wounded animal to a final kill feels what the matador experiences with a bull during the *corrida*.

Soldiers also talk of a "clean kill"—the one-shot kill or, even more rarely, with an edged weapon. But soldiers more often make the judgment to kill on the basis of a perceived danger that demands instant action.

KILLING, HOMICIDE, MURDER

Thou shalt not kill.

—Deuteronomy 5:17; Exodus 20:13

The Sixth Commandment is not ordered for primary attention and seems strange against the background of the bountiful killing for God described in the Hebrew Bible. The Biblical text closely following the prohibition of Deuteronomy 5:17 ordains abundant killing without mercy. Nations such as the Hittites, Girgashites, Amorites, and others are ordained for destruction. There is no contradiction—killing within one's own group is interdicted, it is murder—but the enemy is set out for slaughter. The Sixth Commandment is best translated as "Thou shalt not murder" and could have been expanded beyond the gnomic prohibition to a fuller and accurate version: Thou shalt not kill—except when you have the socially sanctioned privilege for the purpose of protecting your society, as in war or in law enforcement. To do otherwise is to murder—and murder is interdicted. However, when commanded by your nation, you *must* kill, even repeatedly, or you may be cast out, and you may be killed and damned for failure to discharge this responsibility.

Although all people understand that there is a difference between killing and murder, most would have difficulty with the complexity of a formal ethical or legal distinction. A person judged to be guilty of homicide has violated the state's absolute control over use of force. The judgment of "murderer" signifies a lack of an essential aspect of humanity. The killer's life is lessened in value because of his own deed.

Saint Augustine, the first analyst of justified and unjustified killing in the Western tradition, describes as "nonsense" any opposition to killing plants or irrational animals (Saint Augustine 1958). "Thou shalt not kill" applies to man alone. The commandment forbids only self-destruction and, by analogy, killing of other men who are like oneself—one who kills himself, kills a man. But God gives general or specific directions for killing, and the state puts criminals to death according to "rational justice." The soldier is privileged by the state to kill and is, then, "but a sword in hand" and is not personally responsible for the killing and does not violate the commandment.

The killing of *genetically related* people was probably always subject to the most severe proscription. There is early recognition in the Hebrew Bible that nothing is worse than spilling kindred blood. Cain's killing of Abel is primordial homicide (Daly and Wilson 1988), a murder that pollutes society (Jacoby 1983). Augustine's reading of the Sixth Commandment as outlawing self-destruction is not far from the view of the adaptationists who believe that all we are now, body and soul, has been shaped entirely by competition with others for existence and that particular traits are reproduced because they have survival value. The genetic proscription against murder of kindred is a protection against destroying the shared genes—but only from a misinformed perspective that dictates issues of ethnicity and relatedness on the basis of superficial characteristics, such as skin color. From a better-informed point of view, all of humankind is closely related.

Soldiers in national armies are usually not related by blood. Does the genetic regulation of homicide have relevance for war? Is the strong bonding among the non-blood-related brotherhood of modern soldiers attacking an enemy in Vietnam but a reflection of the same "factory-installed" feelings expected in blood-related groups of raiding ancient hominids? In other words, does the situation of war co-opt the genetically determined feelings shaped by adaptation and evolution among nonrelated warriors?

Brotherhood—and the behavior that flows from it—as strong as that of blood ties is forged under conditions of shared stress, as in war. Shakespeare's *Henry*

V stirred his exhausted troops to victory at Agincourt by proclaiming that any man who shed blood with him in battle was to be his brother. The brotherhood among fellow combatants is not exclusively lit by a genetic spark. Culture, civilization, and individual experience reciprocally enfold our DNA, shaping our emotions and behavior toward comrades who share adversity. The soldier's individual experiences, all of what he has read and seen, the sports and the Saturday matinees, all contribute to the brotherhood. The ancient warrior exists in the modern battlefield, less as genetic inheritance than as a ghost, as a powerful metaphor.

KILLING AND MURDER IN WAR

The state exercises its monopoly on mortal force most clearly and consistently in war. Killing by soldiers of other soldiers is not murder unless they violate laws governing the rules of engagement. But growing lists of casualties can cause regulations to be bent or broken. At a time when the Civil War in the United States had gone on for too long with too many killed, General Sherman declared to his soldiers that in their relentless march through the South he wanted the rebels to feel the "hard hand of war" (Grimsley 1995), soldiers and civilians alike. Victory is the primary goal of command, and Sherman made unfeeling force his tool. He allowed his troops to act on their anger toward the rebels by damaging and stealing property. He was indifferent to the suffering brought on the rebels. The carpet and fire bombings of German cities during World War II were deployed more to cripple the Germans' will to continue fighting than to destroy strategic targets.

In a war that has understandable aims, such as survival, we excuse ourselves for violating rules, and the other side is blamed. The Vietnam War continued for too long, and its purpose was not immediately for our survival. As that war continued, violations of the rules of engagement were taken as a further sign of its failed moral purpose. Discovered atrocities led to an increased demand for the war to end and, less vigorously, for the soldiers who had violated regulations to be punished.

Some U.S. soldiers killed women and children. In Vietnam, combatants learned that awaiting orders to fire only after they were certain they were engaging the enemy, who had mortal force, was tantamount to accepting their own death. To delay shooting in order to identify the enemy is part of soldiers' training and includes the soldier's accepting the possibility of his own death as a result (Walzer 1992), but it is a difficult rule to practice or enforce. Soldiers in combat rarely can hold such ascendancy of reason and ethical steadfastness against reflex when under attack. When soldiers cause "collateral damage," that is, killing unarmed civilians, women, and children, they take refuge in the general absolution given all combatants. They hope their friends, the nation, and time will ease their consciences. But the memory of the atrocities committed runs as a continuous painful loop, and they tell it to me to set down a heavy burden.

RESISTANCE TO KILLING

Only one-quarter of American infantrymen in World War II fired their weapons directly at an enemy in their line of sight (Marshall 1947). Soldiers are always reluctant to risk the exposure necessary for returning fire against a visible enemy, but there were other reasons as well. Soldiers wanted to survive, but most ordinary men also resist killing. Despite the constant exhortation to return fire, many did not. Soldiers have fired their weapons partly because that is what they were commanded to do but mainly because their comrades were firing.

Training does not release all soldiers from their resistance to killing. Some small numbers will not fire even when threatened by death. Six thousand of the muskets recovered from the Gettysburg battlefield were found to have multiple rounds in their barrels, some as many as ten. Although double loading could occur by error in the heat of combat, it is also possible that many of the soldiers were averse to killing and so loaded their muskets, mimicked firing, then reloaded another round without firing. Such attitudes are congruent with the behaviors expected in peacetime, and they reassure us about civilization. If we are bred in the bone to kill, it appears that we are also innately resistant to killing (Grossman 1995). There are psychological forces acting within the individual to protect society against killing; there are other forces demanding killing to protect society against its enemies. Killing the enemy to protect the nation is deemed valorous, while running from the slaughter is cowardice, a capital offense with a moral coloring as dark as murder. It is a retreat from what has always been a primarily male duty. To produce a soldier, this internal resistance must be overcome.[1]

The right to manhood has historically been assumed to rest on the ability to kill another man in a just cause. Men who are pressed into service in a shooting war but cannot be taught to kill may be fortunate enough to find posts away from slaughter. They may be good men, good at other things, but if they cannot be aroused to kill to avoid their own death and that of their comrades, they are a detriment to the safety of others. Other men with whom they share mutual dependence will judge them worthless in combat. It is best for all concerned for those who cannot kill to be excused from combat. But those who have avoided fire by any means often feel the need to sew a tuck into their histories, adjust facts, and find justifications for their actions. They often synthesize a fictive personal heroism under fire to protect their manhood.

OVERCOMING RESISTANCE

Military training is meant to wrest the soldier out of the civilian and throw him into action. To do that, training must remove conscripts from the framework of the inhibiting force that civilization has raised against killing. The restraint against mortal force remains deep and pervasive among most combatants at the moment before they kill, even in the well trained. In many soldiers, that innate restraint exerts a stronger force than the fear of their own death. That restraint in our society embodies the central theme of civility. For many soldiers, breaking through that restraint to achieve the soldier's purpose is not easy. Good leaders of platoons know that, and men who become soldiers reluctantly can do a good enough job.

The hierarchy of command directs aggression outside of the group, toward an enemy, reinforcing coherence among the men facing fire. And because aggression and domination form the soldier's group ethos, the inept or incapable soldier is also an enemy. Soft, or nonconforming, men can become victims of collective aggression. When they are forced out or killed, other combatants can be relieved. If they die, their deaths are not mourned. The survivors are better off without them and better able to do the soldier's job.

THE ENEMY "DESPECIATED"

A declaration of war involves, among other things, a process by which the state assigns a lowered human value to the enemy, and in a war against an enemy identified as a separate racial group, the value is likely to be reduced to nonhuman: "You see those dinks, they've got nothing, no cars, nothing, living in a grass shack, shit they ain't human" (R.T.). Soldiers kill "gooks," "dinks," "slants." On the other side, our enemy kill "big noses" or "the great Satan." Such dehumanization, or "despeciation," by representing a part for the whole, helps overcome the moral dictates against killing by declaring the enemy to be alien and subhuman, and that is the prelude to atrocity. The trick to *dehumanization* occurs when one focuses on a perceived characteristic of the other—to separate that person from one's own group or nation. This characteristic is used as though it was a total description of the human being. Skin color, eye configuration—any characteristic can be inflated to mean the totality; that is, a *synecdoche*, a figure of speech in which the part represents the whole.

WAR ITSELF DEMEANS

What Clausewitz (1984) called the "penetrating showers of excitement" is found in killing. It is made intense by the clarity found in facing mortal danger. The innate resistance to killing, however, brought from home, derived from the mutual enfolding of culture and evolution, is countered by the demand of combat to kill, to protect those at home and comrades at one's side. This antinomy is played out in the soldier at war, but the closeness of men at arms reduces or eliminates that hesitation imposed by the soldier's internal conflict.

A helicopter gunner in Vietnam, raised to be a "God-fearing Christian," says that he realized early, like the others who survived, that he had to kill the enemy or he and his friends would die. Combat revealed to him that the politics or justness of his nation's cause, even his religious training, had little relevance to the immediate mortal actuality. He and his buddies killed from "Chinooks" (large helicopters), but they also took great risks to pick up Vietnamese villagers and their animals to remove them from danger. He and other crew members started and supported a home for orphan children. Other American combatants did the same. As a psychological necessity, they had to separate and compartmentalize their opposing emotions to restore meaning.

This gunner felt the excitement in killing and suffered guilt for liking it. He attempted to counter the way in which war demeaned him by protecting some part of what was important to him before the war. He was entirely aware of the inconsistency, but living through war and surviving physically, morally, and spiritually meant living with it. There was mutual support in the gunship crew. In what has often been called "the dark heart of war," he and his friends attempted to protect a part of themselves from the killing they were doing (G. Offringa, personal communication).

WEAPONS

I have no words
My voice is in my sword.

—Shakespeare, *Macbeth*

Killing once depended on strength of arm and resolve in the chancy skills needed to use edged weapons. The development of firearms made training with horse, sword, and lance less important and killing more democratic, open to all men with a gun. The Colt handgun that "won the West" was known as "the equalizer"; that name became a generic for firearms, representing equal-opportunity killing.

At the beginning of the twentieth century, a soldier typically had to fire off his own weight in bullets to injure an enemy; personal weapons are now far more effective (Dunnigan 1988). Technological innovation has increased the individual soldier's safety by increasing the distance at which he can direct effective fire. Technology removes the soldier from personal involvement. It removes the passion from killing, and the soldier may feel less guilty responsibility. There is a concomitant reduction in the emotional consequences of violence associated with close-up and personal combat (O'Connell 1989). Killing at a distance with missiles or from a gunship can become routinized and performed with little emotional attachment and with less hyperalertness, disturbing thoughts, or dreams experienced afterward: "air sports," one gunship pilot called it (Herr 1968).

Watching the flight of smart missiles on a video screen homing in on their targets is as engaging as a video game. In the ultimate professional description of electronically monitored and guided slaughter, a contemporary military commander says they do not kill the enemy, "we service targets" (Martinez 2004).

The personal weapons of ground soldiers are traditionally designated as "light," meaning that the weapons and ammunition can be carried by the soldier without assistance. In Vietnam, the M-16A assault weapon fired a small-caliber

(5.56 mm) round, a fraction smaller in size than .22 caliber but with far greater velocity than conventional civilian rifles of the target/hunting variety. The bullets tumble in flight and tear a large hole in a body. These weapons can be switched to fully automatic, to rock and roll, and the thirty-round magazine can be fired off in less than three seconds. Infantrymen can carry no more than a dozen M-16 magazines, but firefights did not last long enough to exhaust the grunt's supply of "caps."[2] Hand-thrown grenades and grenade and rocket launchers supplement the personal assault weapons for an infantry platoon. Some soldiers carry handguns, of questionable help in a firefight, and a bayonet, most useful for opening cans in these days of long-distance killing (Dunnigan 1988). Along with that array of light weapons, the American soldier in Vietnam could also call for an air strike and bring down an enormous potential force on an enemy. Weapons extend the soldier emotionally—far beyond the limit of his body—but he is dehumanized into a weapon; he dreams of himself as a weapon (D.K.).

THE MAGIC OF WEAPONS

Firing a weapon excites, and can strangely soothe: "You know what it's like to fire an AK47? It's . . . a high! I could just fire one clip after another and watch the target blow away. No, I never killed anything with it but it would be so easy [smiles]" (twenty-four-year-old gun enthusiast, not a former combatant).

One reporter from a liberal political publication, working on a story about gun schools in Los Angeles, wrote that after she was talked into firing a gun at the pistol range: "I discovered a curious thing: I liked it" (Ladowsky 1992). "When I feel antsy, I load up an automatic and blow away a target, or stuff off my porch . . . It calms me down" (V.E., a veteran living in rural isolation).

Action at a distance is magical. Automatic weapons engage the destructive desire to unleash irresistible force. The desire becomes an all-engrossing fact; force is "launched from the eyes"—the eye sees, the missile flies its trajectory, annihilates space, and the opponent who would kill you is dead. "It's magic," says a soldier talking about a "kill at a 'klick' [kilometer] . . . Now you see it, now you don't" (V.E.). Killing the man who wants to kill you erases the primal fear of death. The repetitive exercise of such control and dominance over terror becomes addictive, and other experience pales.

KILLING EMBRACED

It is well that war is so terrible, we would grow too fond of it.

—General Robert E. Lee to General Longstreet, an aide at Fredericksburg[3]

Combatants who have killed talk about passing through a felt resistance, a palpable barrier to killing during combat. For many men, there may not be happiness in killing, but there is something related to satisfaction.

Dr.: What did you like about Vietnam?

R.T.: Exciting . . . stuff coming in . . . whoosh . . . bam-bam. (very excitedly) Oh, I got to really liking the killing!

A thirty-year-old U.S. Army veteran of the Gulf War, born in Vietnam of Vietnamese parents, describes a childhood of fear in his native country. "I had made a promise to myself that I would stay away from war . . . No war, no more killing. Then I did it, I joined up. I went to war and I liked it, the killing, I mean. Something is very the matter with me" (O.G.).

A German soldier in Russia during World War II wrote of the "drunken exhilaration which follows fear . . . inducing both sides to commit inconceivable atrocities . . . an overwhelming desire for destruction" (Sajer 1967, p. 234).

The soldier in a state of highest arousal acts and kills with satisfaction at the result. With the danger over and the enemy dead or subdued, a deep calm can follow. Combat focuses the terrors of helplessness onto the real mortal enemy and effective action erases those terrors.

A combat veteran held a thief with his gun until the police arrived. He tells of it in arresting detail, and then comments: "I had not felt as good, sure, and calm since Vietnam" (V.E.).

That past killing can be held as a pleasurable reminiscence is rarely noted in the vast literature on the psychic aftermath of the Vietnam War. Yet it is known that many veterans experienced satisfaction in killing and, through memories of killing and slaughter, rekindle some of the pleasure of the event.

But former soldiers can be profoundly troubled by their fixation on violence and the dissonance between what they are thinking and what is appropriate. For some soldiers, the nature of the war in Vietnam and, they fear, their own nature, carried them beyond defined civilized limits, and they cannot find those limits within themselves again.

KILLING UP CLOSE

A soldier who was in combat in Vietnam at the beginning of the war describes how the bullet that was meant to kill him marked the point at which the war became real. He relives his experience in therapy: while on patrol he discovers a Vietnamese man hiding along a trail:

> I didn't react at first; give people a chance I thought. Anyway we had orders, then, not to shoot if they were unarmed, you get a court martial for that . . . I motioned with my hand to come out but he kept backing up into the brush and I moved toward him still motioning . . . Suddenly he brings up a carbine he had hidden in his pants, so I fire, try to fire my M-16 and it jammed! I take his round in my face—but I was just lucky enough to be behind a dike—I dropped my head down and I don't know how I did it, but I pulled back on the bolt, cleared the chamber and came back up firing at him. He was maybe five feet away. I emptied the whole magazine into him, and the medics came up . . . I was spurting blood onto my arm from my face. I was never so angry, I can't describe it, totally crazy out of control; they had to pull me away. I had my K-bar out to put a knife into him also . . . and he was already in shreds, like a doll a dog had gotten into. His hands were shredded, fingers snapped off—he must have put his hands up to his head . . . After that, I was different; I wouldn't give anyone a chance. Calmer, funny to say—but because I knew what I had to do to stay alive, better than those guys who were telling me what to do . . . I wasn't going to give anybody a second chance to kill me. (R.O.)

The soldier is calmed and satisfied by subduing an enemy who would have done the same to him. But those experiences are never forgotten and return in thoughts that trouble his sleep. Those rekindled events counter his feelings of vulnerability long after the war is over.

The *enemy* is usually a mass, not distinguishable as an individual. But when a soldier is close to the enemy soldier he has just killed, the psychological strategy of denying the opponent his humanity may fail.

KILLING IN SEXUAL EMBRACE

I will kill thee and love thee after.

—William Shakespeare, *Othello*

Killing within the reach of "sexual embrace" increases the physical and mental involvement and maximizes the danger to the killer (Grossman 1995). In such an embrace, "up close and personal," a soldier can smell the man he is about to kill and sometimes can see how the "light leaves his eyes." Killing with an edged weapon takes skill, resolve, and strength—luck is of lesser consequence. The prospect of killing up close is fearfully anticipated by all but a few. But it is part of the mythology of war that a soldier is only truly initiated, "blooded," baptized by war, after killing at closest quarters with an edged weapon. Although it is difficult for most soldiers to think about killing with a knife or bayonet, to feel the wound as it is made, and to see blood staining the weapon's edge, there are soldiers who seek or learn to seek that mortal contest with another man.

That moment before the soldier delivers death up close is fulsome in anticipation of the next instant. It is action at its highest level because it is in extreme contrast to the person about to be voided by force, "his death is upon him, but not dead" (Shakespeare, *Anthony and Cleopatra*, act 4, scene 15).

> I came up behind this sentry, a kid, must have been a VC-FNG (a fucking new guy, an inexperienced, new recruit) because he was moving too much. I had my bayonet and I grabbed him from behind and he felt the blade against his neck and he sagged before I cut him, like he was dead before I killed him. I then put the bayonet through the back of his neck and jammed it up into his skull and into his brain, then I used the bayonet as a handle to lie him slowly down on the ground . . . I remember that moment, before taking him, in silence, in slow motion. I'll remember that forever. (V.E.)

He says that he drinks coffee to remember all the details. He rarely drinks coffee otherwise; he is already hyperalert and concerned about being too much out of control. But the coffee helps to re-create the "details" that are, paradoxically, soothing. Without these memories of danger, routine peacetime gives him a desperate feeling of isolation and anomie.

He is a weapons expert, who is aroused and calmed by movies and by books about the war or frequent talk with other veterans. He would rather face an enemy than feel the closeness of a friend; that becomes a continuing, often desperate, struggle for him.

The act of "taking" a man with a knife is often experienced with sexual excitement. There is total possession in such killing. For men who want to do it and have done it, the remembered experience is often "taped" into memory, deeply satisfying and consciously re-evoked. That does not indicate a severe character aberration; it is too common.

Although the bayonet is now rarely used as a combat weapon, it is still a part of the foot soldiers' indoctrination into the military life. It remains because, among those who train others for combat, there is the persistent view that a soldier trained to be resolute with a knife will not pull back from killing (Dunnigan 1988).[4]

Only some soldiers catch the "spirit of the bayonet" and penetrate their own psychological barrier to "push it home" through muscle, gristle, and bone. The Marines talk of "burying the knife": "Nobody can bury the knife unless they have felt the pain, that is, had a friend killed—or taken a hit himself" (R.O.). "Without that, you hesitate. You don't bury the knife unless it is the only thing in your head, you feel the surge in your whole body, and you can only want to bury it in him. 'Want' isn't the right word—getting him is *all there is* of the world" (E.P.).

There is a psychological barrier to thrusting a knife directly into an enemy. Men in training often continue to try to use the edge of the bayonet fixed to the end of their rifle despite the instruction that slashing is ineffective. Soldiers want to slash at an enemy rather than to thrust the steel into him; that way they can avoid the closer and more prolonged contact that comes with a head-on attack. Soldiers in the Army Special Forces, in contrast, are schooled in the use of the deadly thrust from behind; it surprises; it is silent, quicker, surer, and more lethal (Grossman 1995). If the face and eyes of the victim are not visible, then the emotional strain on the perpetrator may be lessened, and there is less hesitation to strike home.

MAN BECOMES WEAPON

> Now, I am become death, shatterer of worlds.
>
> —Robert J. Oppenheimer, quoting from the *Bhagavad-gita*,
> on witnessing the world's first nuclear explosion

Weapons become a part of the body of soldiers. That is not only a metaphor. The infantryman cleans, caresses, sleeps with his rifle—sometimes masturbates with it. Each recruit in the U.S. military distinguishes his personal weapon as a "rifle," or a "piece" (of ordnance) but never a "gun." "Gun" is a word used only by civilians. He repeats the doggerel learned from his sergeant: "Here is my weapon; here is my piece" and with gestures demonstrates that he must call both the rifle and his penis a "weapon" or "piece."

Front Towards Enemy

—An instruction cast into the face of the Claymore mine,
an antipersonnel mine with a guaranteed casualty area fifty yards long

The boy becomes soldier, grown old in combat, becomes one with war. He is in it; it is within him. He does not feel it as something alien. The continued use of force is addictive; it erases others feelings and can "turn the man into stone"— it makes a man into a weapon. Such a soldier thinks like the enemy, knows what they know. He is the war.

A Marine psychologically damaged by war reminisced about Vietnam, the long past still present: "I sit there, in the rain, rocking back and forth . . . I've got a sort of smile on my face, because I know, I know, and the guys back there in the dry, in bunkers or covered by their ponchos, they don't know . . . I don't put my poncho over me to stay dry and warm. They [the enemy] hear that [rain hitting the poncho] . . . and I don't feel wet or cold, I feel nothing . . . It's like I'm a Claymore just sitting there, rain sliding off of me and not feeling it, not moving, waiting, ready" (E.P).

At the end of World War II, as part of Germany's final attempt to destroy England's will, V1 and V2 rockets were launched against England. There was also a plan to launch Bachem Vipers, small aircraft without landing gear or the usual technical instruments. They were to be loaded with explosives and flown by their human pilots to the enemy, where target, plane, and pilot would be vaporized as one. More than were needed volunteered for this squadron. Suicide bombing persists as a disturbing tactic of war.

SAVAGE AMUSEMENT

Not necessity, not desire. No, the love of power is the demon of men.

—Friedrich Nietzsche, *Beyond Good and Evil*

There are those who really like killing or discover that they do. Once the barrier is breached, killing can become an excursion into freedom without boundaries. That has been true in past wars, and some men express a wish for such freedom and welcome war as the open door to it.

Wyndham Lewis was a member of the English artistic prowar Vorticist Movement before World War I and espoused the nobility to be found in denying the instinct for self-survival. Although he had never been in combat, he wrote, "Killing somebody must be the greatest pleasure in existence: either like killing yourself without being interfered with by the instinct of self-preservation or exterminating the instinct of self-preservation itself" (Hynes 1991, pp. 9–10). Destruction has an esthetic side that it borrows from its opposite, that is, from creation. The power of killing exerted in war resembles what an artist does when he violates boundaries, takes liberties with expectations, shows the darkest side of human affairs, makes comedy of the most somber. But loving killing is opposite to the joy of artistic creativity in the way that sexual coercion or perversion is to *its* opposite, that is, loving.

THE END OF KILLING

The ritual celebrations and parades at the end of war are meant to rebind the soldier to the expected, to the ordinary, and to separate him from the taint of blood. Peace brings a cessation of war's horrors, but soldiers' most enduring connection remains to past comradeship in the intoxicating, ecstatic mixture of savagery and love found only in war and now only in memory. Reacculturation for peace was missing in the immediate post-Vietnam era. There were none of those customary and necessary "expiatory rituals" (Bataille 1986) immediately following Vietnam.

One returned Marine proposed, with general assent from his friends, that they might have had lessened emotional burdens if returning Vietnam soldiers had been sent back to a training camp before discharge for a "deconditioning" program with a schedule of gradually decreasing the firing of weapons. What they really needed, Vietnam veterans say, was to be allowed to return in a prolonged "welcome back." Instead, "processing out of country" was fast and furious. Seventy-two hours after the killing, a soldier could be found sitting down to dinner in peaceful Peoria, with his father asking about his future employment plans.

Separation from service is no surprise, but it is a shock. One man said he felt as if he were propelled into the air with no hands reaching out to catch him. Family was of no help, and he knew that his wife could not possibly understand. "They should have just left us in 'Nam. We were used up and knew that we could have no life, beyond what we already had. After all the killing, we should have been left to die in Vietnam" (E.P.).

KILLERS

BRED IN THE BONE

I was the King of Death . . .
Nothing matters to the King of Death.
—D.K.

Only a few men became true killers in Vietnam and got caught up in the magic of wielding full-bore, overwhelming force. Most of them had been ordinary men. Before they had their war, very few of them contemplated killing as reality. Even fewer had thought the unthinkable, that they would find satisfaction and excitement in taking human life. Combat bent and broke the boundaries of the ordinary and expected, altered many of these men permanently, damaged them for peace, not only through the horrors they saw but also because of its repeated wonder of their real and potential power. Some combatants captured in what has been referred to as the "dark heart of war and its beauty" wanted to stay on and had to be forced to leave Vietnam. Many men stayed in Vietnam past their time because they did not want to leave their comrades. Some stayed because of the addictive nature of the killing, because they "could not get enough war" (D.K.).

God's proscription against slaughter is textured by the exceptions allowing religious, tribal, or national sanctions for killing (as noted in chapter 3). But there is a further supplement: "and thou shalt not find pleasure or satisfaction in it." Yet all of us could imagine the satisfaction in killing an enemy determined to kill us. The sanctioned use of mortal force enthralls the susceptible man. A man who has been exposed to repeated killing can lose his boundaries and become a killer in combat. Although many veterans care little about the fact of killing, which was accepted because it was necessary, many veterans are morally concerned about killing because they liked the "high" they felt when they killed. One veteran wonders if he killed more, and unnecessarily, because he liked the killing (S.V.). Killing generates its own power of attraction: "It gets away from you" (V.E.). Most men possess the capacity to kill, and it can be kindled by training and war. Few Vietnam combatants, however, thought of themselves as "born killers"; very few started training for combat in Asia with a single passion for inflicting mortal harm. The number of "killers" among soldiers in World War II, those who sought out opportunities to kill because they liked it, was about 2 percent (Swank and Marchand 1946; Grossman 1995).

Killer soldiers are more dangerous to their fighting unit than to the enemy. Killers damage the cohesiveness of a fighting unit (F. Downs and G. Offringa, personal communication). A killer soldier's presence wears away at the tether that keeps men in combat connected to a larger, although distant, idea of civilization and the rule of law governing individual behavior in war. Such soldiers can also bring death to others in their group; they are restless behind the lines, seek contact, and are incautious (Gray 1970).

Killers are identified within combat units, and good leaders attempt to isolate them. The usual soldier keeps his distance from the killer and does not regard him as a hero (Grossman 1995).

Fred Downs was a platoon leader in Vietnam and is the author of books on combat.[1] Downs believes that the war was prosecuted mostly by men who were drafted into service but were "professionals" because of the way they managed their responsibility and their lives in combat. They were "dependable men who know what they were there for, learned the tough job, and did it" (F. Downs, interview). They were not there for heroics, but they gave all they had. There were also "regular guys" who soldiered adequately and with minimal complaint. They took the grisly job as theirs to do and did it as best they could.

The other two groups that Downs identified were "misfits," men who cannot function in combat and try to avoid it, and the "psychokillers," who looked for opportunities to kill, took pleasure in destruction and repeatedly violated the rules of engagement. Downs was tolerant of those not suited for war but he wanted the killers out of his platoon. Pleasure and excitement in killing have little utility in modern war and is dangerous to those who want to do their job and finish it. It can deflect a group's attention away from their mission. It tarnishes the purity of arms. Downs sees "real killers" as bred in the bone:

> There were a few people who enjoyed the killing, and they were as dangerous to us as they were to the enemy—they were nuts. I tried to get rid of them. Then you had those who were really good at the job. I mean, they just did it—real professionals even though they were young men and had been in combat only a couple of months . . . They did it—it was their job. They were solid, dependable. They . . . had trouble with the killing—it bothered them. Killing a person far away was not so bad, but when the person was closer, it became very difficult for them. . . . Let's say you captured someone—if your psycho tried to torture or beat up on the prisoner, the majority of the platoon, which were the average guys, and even the professionals to a certain extent—they wouldn't allow that—they'd stop it because they saw the other man as a soldier and there was no need for this. It was only the psycho or the person having trouble who would do the torturing and do the other things. There was no reason for it. If there was . . . information that you needed that was important to you that meant your survival, then, in that case, they'd turn a head . . . to get the job done but there had to be a reason for it and it had to do with your own survival or survival of your compadres.

The ordinary loving men who discover their attachment to war (Broyles 1984) are not killers "bred in the bone" who find war somehow and couple with it. "Natural-born killers" are rare, different from other soldiers. It is as if they have been waiting for the hammer and heat of combat to shape them fully; it is as if they have been programmed in their genes to kill (Herr 1977). Those men easily become one with war's force and are reluctant to leave it.

One veteran no longer wants the characterization he placed on himself as a "killer." Intelligent and well read, he sees his past as shaped by a disinterested, often cruel father and a family that he rejected before adolescence. He is unable to work because of severe physical disability from an automobile accident:

> I wanted to be a Marine since age 12 . . . I was meant for it . . . Where else can you get paid to kill? I wanted combat . . . went out looking for firefights . . . Combat turned on a switch in me that can't be shut off.
>
> I go into a room even now and I look around for objects that can be turned into weapons. I can make things you wouldn't think of into a killing weapon . . . I want to stop, because I cannot be normal, cannot have love. (V.E.)

He describes to his doctor how he could use a book or pen on the desk or even a drinking straw as a weapon. He cannot stop thinking about mortal attack, and he is deeply troubled that he still talks about it, not only to his therapist but also to his friends and to young people, who become uncomfortable in his presence. He knows that they call him "weird," but he takes some satisfaction in the unquiet he creates. He wants others to know that in a fight he would die rather than surrender and that he will endure any injury to kill an enemy. That is the major part of his morality "as a warrior." He demands respect for it, and it distinguishes him from civilians.

His feeling for mortal contact sounds like love. He describes the actions of a much-decorated Marine in Vietnam, Sergeant Hathcock, whom he had met and read about. Hathcock had been using a fifty-caliber machine gun, fitted with a telescopic scope, as a sniper weapon. The fifty caliber has a slow rate of fire, and a single round can easily be fired.

In combat in Vietnam, he had been sighting this weapon in on a waterfall. A Vietcong soldier stopped at that waterfall for a drink: "God, I love it! He had just sighted the weapon on that spot! He squeezes off one round from the 'fifty' and the 780-grain hardball projectile flies its flat parabola and vaporizes that guy. You know that is a shot in a thousand—just sighted on that spot. I would have loved to have been there or better to have done it" (V.E.).[2]

This veteran's narratives often linger on the details of the fulsome moments before the kill, the trajectory of the bullet certain of its target, savored in slow motion. He regains arousal, power, and uniqueness when he tells of how he could easily maim or kill the listener. He admits that he looks for the flicker of fear in his doctor's eyes. He has lived an extraordinary life, and he wants honor for it. He defies "judgments [of worth] made by civilians." He has met exacting standards where the outcome was absolute; civilians, he knows, cannot comprehend the level of contest at which he is proficient.

He is older and now wants to stop such thoughts and feelings, but he has great difficulty surrendering his warrior's stance to prevail over the pressure of peacetime judgment. Mortal combat remains at his emotional center and his perceptions, and he continues to yearn for the focused arousal state he once found in war. He is uncomfortable and frustrated with such longing, never fully satisfied in reminiscences. With time and effort, the intensity of those needs slowly decreases.

For most ordinary men who are not born to kill, it is possible that the intense excitement generated by carnage will dazzle them. Such men do not commit atrocities repeatedly, but they can get pulled into it during combat and find it exciting; at that moment, they are intoxicated and pulled into destruction. Good men are, thereafter, tortured by memories of what they have done or witnessed. They are shocked by the electric thrill, or what has been called "satisfaction" felt in killing (Gray 1970).

> Words can't describe it, or jeez, maybe someone from Harvard could find the right word. It is like you feel it in your whole body, always high, a screaming high, juiced, pumped. All the time, not just in [the] middle of contact. Some guy will shit his pants, when nothing is going down. It is like you are outside of yourself, you got to do it, got to get back at [the enemy], and you know, right away without thinking, how to do it as nasty as you can. You set up an ambush and everyone knows what to do, [set up sticks] for fields of fire, everything. You want to put craters in them [enemies], not just little holes—and then you can say to them when they are down—[smile] did you like that? . . . I got you, I'm here, you're dirt. It's like you've got some reflex that just goes off, and when you finally do it, kill, hurt them a thousand times more than they did you, and you feel, maybe for a minute—that it is all OK, all right and you feel it's right, maybe for a minute. All the pumped-up feeling, all the electricity comes in that little minute. (E.P.)

That is true for most combatants. Some combatants bring anger with them to battle. A much-decorated seventy-seven-year-old Filipino soldier, a sniper who fought through the entire World War II European campaign, says it similarly: "Talking . . . words, that is nothing. Only killing eased the hurt and then gave the satisfaction. I'm angry, I've been so angry all the time. I brought my rage [from family abuse] to Europe and the war. I raged, I raged. Every German in the sights of my rifle is dead. I kill, and that feels better for a while. But it gets away from you" (S.F.).

Although some men go to combat consumed with rage that drives them to kill, no evidence exists of a "killing" trait, or attribute, buried in the precombat personality of most soldiers who become excited by killing. War and its exuberant freedom from restraint and sudden terrifying losses spark the explosion into killing lust. Soldiers are excited about getting back at the enemy with successful counterforce. Yet even with combat's incomparable excitement, most men would live out their lives without the enthrallment of killing.

LOOSENING OF RESTRAINT

The Vietnam War stretched the envelope of "just" rules designed to control the actions of soldiers. With time, our nation lost the semblance of goals and valid political and military reason for continuing the war (Sheehan 1988). Body counts of Vietcong were pumped up and thrust forward to impersonate coherent purpose. There was no front, and villages once "pacified" could dangerously change allegiance. The war's incoherence affected the men on the ground, lessened the claim of rules and standards, and, in that, further demeaned them. Killing—the body counts—became command's purpose because they had no other, and for many ordinary soldiers, killing became their purpose, too.

In war, many men seek a sense of "nobility," a way of rising above the demeaning aspects of combat by killing and dominating other men. That may have been more the case in the Vietnam War. Soldiers killed to survive, less for any positive cause other than to escape what one combatant (R.M.) described as a personal feeling of "deadness" in that war. Combat veterans said of themselves that in Vietnam as adolescents they were "lords of death," "kings," "gods" (Bradshaw, Ohlde, and Hjorne 1991; Nadelson 1992). Now close to or into their sixth decade, some continue to long for the feeling of transcendence they found in the war or "which found them" (R.M). They would like to believe that they acted in consonance with the nature of the war, but some still are deeply troubled by the thought that it rose out of a profound defect in their own character. Many register deepest sadness about what they became in war and also speak with great clarity about what the availability of force did to them:

Dr.: Did you think about killing before you joined the Marines?

E.P.: No—never before . . . Once you have had that, though, it is in you, it is you . . . When you call in an air strike, you say you "can see them," you tell them you can see VC [Vietcong], you say, so many of my people are down. You say, "requesting an air strike," you give the coordinates, you wait—and you feel the rush as it comes in like magic, like God's thunder . . . rolls over you, past you, through you, and toward them, you feel that power inside yourself, that unbelievable rush, and you're a part of that, that's coming from you. It's like touching the hem of His robe or something.

LIKING THE KILLING

> For I'll not kill thee there, nor there, nor there . . .
> I'll kill thee every where, yea, o'er and o'er.
>
> —William Shakespeare, *Troilus and Cressida*

Sanctioned killing can intoxicate men, and surprisingly, even in cultures where there is little or no aggression, men can be taught to kill. Among the tribe of the Semai Senoi of Southeast Asia, Dentan writes, there is no concept of violence against another and no word for killing. There was no homicide, no physical attacks of one tribe member against another; children were not struck, and chickens were beheaded as a sad necessity. The British Army, however, conscripted Semai men in the 1950s, gave them uniforms, and trained and armed them for counterinsurgency. When they returned to the Semai society, they reverted to nonviolence and dissociated from their war experience. In the war, however, they had become eager killers. Here is a typical Semai veteran's story: "We killed, killed, killed. The Malays would stop and go through people's pockets and take their watches and money. We only thought of killing. Wah, truly we were drunk with blood." One man even described how he had drunk the blood of the man he had killed (Dentan 1968).

A veteran said that as he looked at the bodies of the Vietnamese soldiers his platoon had just killed in ambush, he "wanted to do it again and again" (N.S.). Bodies were mutilated by both sides in the most savage ways. One veteran of Vietnam says: "Christ, I got off on it, killing . . . I did it because I was angry; I did it because I was bored. We would collect ears . . . Like we would write on our flak jackets, 'Make war not love.' After that I knew I'd rather fight than screw. I sure didn't think that way, ever, before the war" (R.T.). In Vietnam, a Marine licked his enemy's blood from his knife (Herr 1977).

The danger of being overrun—the enforced passivity before engagement—agitates men beyond comparison and demands assertion of mastery. Such feelings, especially if leadership is poor or weak, can move the susceptible to atrocity. Once the killing started, soldiers could not break cohesion with their friends—they killed together. Love, as Tim O'Brien points out, can also pull soldiers into evil (O'Brien 1994). Studies by psychologist Stanley Milgram demonstrated just how vulnerable "normals" are to the encouragement to inflict pain on their peers (Milgram 1963).

THE KING OF DEATH

Dogs, would you live forever?

—Frederick the Great, exhorting his troops toward sacrifice for victory

Many veterans talk of their present disconnection to our world—the civilian rules and the social "dance" after combat. One veteran, when he describes the changes war in Vietnam made in him, surprises me with the word "grace." He refers to a photograph of him in a camp away from combat. He says, "It is all there, what I had, in my face, in that smile." He brought in the enlarged photograph for me to see:

E.P.: I have something no one here could or will know. I don't want them [family] to hang that [photograph] in the house. They don't know what it means, can never know, and you can't tell them. I couldn't explain it to them, and I have to stop short of trying; it starts to get them messed up. But if they really understood, it would really mess them up.

Dr.: Can you say it?

E.P.: Well, I had the—what I call grace. I earned it. It wasn't easy and it won't disappear.

Dr.: Say some more.

E.P.: Well, an unbelievable power you can't believe, like that [force] I got calling in the air strike and seeing that ordnance going out. My God, that power you could bring down, like from heaven. I can see it in the photo; I can see it, and other veterans who look at that picture would know it also—nobody else. I had grace.

Dr.: Grace?

E.P.: Power, force. I could take anything I wanted. If I wanted something I could have it.

Dr.: Would you kill . . . for it?

E.P.: Sure easy . . . If I wanted to—that can of peaches was mine, everyone knew not to fuck with me, they could [see it in my eyes]. What I wanted was mine, it was there on my face.

Dr.: Your face said it more than a weapon.

E.P.: That's it. But I would die for one of my buddies. I could, I would, they did for me. That was grace.

Dr.: What is 'it' and 'grace'?

E.P.: I think that I just said it, I don't know what to call it. I call it grace, I can see it in some others, R [*another veteran*] has it. Grace comes out of . . . not worrying about continuing your life. Like you come on the feeling that you have the permission to do it. It comes from you or maybe from God—the permission to do what you want, even to giving up your life. Knowing, really knowing what you want, whatever it is, right now—clear, sharp, no waver—that is really living. Certain that you always could at any time give up your life for what you really wanted. You didn't think about it, it was there, it was you. And anything you wanted, you wanted hard . . . It came to me that I was ready to die for what I wanted, go up against a guy who, shit, wanted—my can of peaches or was going to kill me or my buddy. I didn't think it up, figure it out, it came to me and I have never said it before in words: I could give up my life, like that, no hesitation, for friends or for what I wanted. That's what I had. I could die to get what I wanted. I could take being killed if it was to kill that other guy, or save a buddy. That's power, that's freedom—that's grace.

That's it, that's it! That's what it takes. That is much more than the weapon you carry. It's the will! The sureness of yourself comes from knowing you can give up your life to get what you want. Not caring about your own life puts you in charge of it, not afraid of your life. I mean not afraid to lose it. It makes you so sure of yourself that you become a King of Death—and of Life too—I mean that is grace, close to being God . . . It is being God . . . [*quietly*] Oh God, forgive me.

The boy's anxiety about proving himself disappeared—a sleight of hand performed when he went to Asia. No fear of God or a father who judges individual acts and assigns destinies. He keeps it secret because that memory of the feeling of "grace" is precious and could be ridiculed, tampered with by peacetime values, and he has no argument with which to defend its meaning.

What he says about "grace" restates that strand in our history that accords nobility to those men ready to sacrifice their lives to achieve and maintain domination over other men. They have grace, permission to do that. On the larger scale, the ability and will to kill and dominate to gain such power has been a major force shaping human history. For the individual, the experience is seductive, yes, liberating, and it can drive men to seek more killing. It is a hook, a needle.

FORCE AND SUBMISSION

Sing, goddess, the anger of Peleus's son, Achilles

and its devastation, which put pains thousand fold upon the Achaians.

—Homer, *The Iliad*

The Western world's first full historical narrative is about men killing men in war. Simone Weil's essay on the *Iliad*, which was written as the *Wehrmacht* occupied Paris, begins by shifting focus away from the person of Achilles: "The true hero, the true subject of the Iliad is force . . . The man who is the possessor of force seems to walk through a nonresistant element; in the human substance that surrounds him nothing has the power to interpose between the impulse and the act, the tiny interval that is reflection. Force is that factor that turns anybody who is subjected to it into a thing," and Weil notes that the soldier, after killing, becomes a nonsentient force himself (Weil 1985). Force is central to the male idea of war. Force, potential and actual, has been at the interface between men and women (Shay 1994). It is also at the nations' boundaries.

BEAUTY, *DUENDE*

In the *Iliad*, Patroclus, an Achaian (Greek) hero, kills a Trojan in motion, coming abreast of his chariot and gaffing him as he would a fish—cleanly, elegantly, spectacularly. Patroclus's adroitness and extraordinary (if not quite believable) level of physical control eclipse the grotesque and transfigure that killing into an esthetic act, the killer into an artist.

[*Patroclus*] stabbed his right jawbone,

ramming the spearhead square between his

teeth so hard

he hooked him by that spearhead over the

chariot rail,

hoisted, dragged the Trojan out as an

angler perched

on a jutting rock ledge drags some fish

from the sea,

some noble catch with line and

glittering bronze hook

So with the spear Patroclus gaffed him

off his car,

his mouth gaping round the glittering

point

and flipped him down face first

dead as he fell, his life breath

blown away.

And next he caught Erylaus closing,

lunging in

he flung a rock and it struck between

his eyes

and man's whole skull split in his heavy

helmet,

down the Trojan slammed on the ground,

head down

and courage-shattering Death engulfed

his corpse.

—Homer 1990, 16.479–94

We can be repelled by killing force; yet, it rivets us (Homer 1990), particularly if performed elegantly. The ancient poet moves the reader to admire the killer's easy proficiency, like a sniper taking down a man at great distance, bring[ing] "the dark . . . whirling down across his eyes" (Homer 1990, book 4, line 534, p. 160) similarly jolts our attention.

There is joy and celebration of the killer's own life, skillfully taking a life. He is the hunter or, in the simile, the fisherman, the superior of the slain, the quick and not the dead. He is the manifest lord, raised high by the dead body he has created. The victim is face down, neutered, dirtied, and diminished. The killer has manifested the most naked self-assertion. He is lasciviousness personified. He is adulated as a hero, his potency glorified; he shines. The elegance of killing action in war is celebrated throughout the Greek tragedies; it is echoed in the Hebrew Bible (Niditch 1993) and in literature on war through history. Ordinary men exposed to war can feel exultant and simultaneously fearful about what war has raised in them. A small number of other men, the killers among soldiers, never become sated.

A *matador*, who possesses what the Spanish call *duende*, creates Homeric death in the afternoon through confident action. He exposes his body to mortal risk in order to kill the bull with grace and to give those who watch a vision of the transcendence of a man over the brute, of the aesthetic over the grimness of death. At his very best, the matador who achieves the height of his craft and art is in control of his own fear as well as of the bull. He moves us, but as the bull rushes past him, he does not move; he is unmoved. He rises above the bloody sand of the arena floor; he stands apart from the killing. In the filth of combat, there can be similar killing, the terror of an encounter with the enemy becomes suddenly extraordinary. A Marine says:

> The first time I killed, I bungled, used two clips . . . butchered him. I went to look at him and I threw up. Later, I was waiting in ambush and a VC came toward me, and I hit him with a single round in the chest and he fell back—I mean the round shoved him back— arms limp and unfolding, he went back, head turning [he does the movements], slow . . . like a ballet dancer. After that I could do it, like—bam, bam, bam—four quick shots and they kick back, unfold, their hands, fingers do this. [He imitates a sudden then languid opening of his hands and a falling back of his head to the side.] I did that, it's a wonder. It was beautiful.
>
> Did you hear what I just said? "Beautiful," how could I say that, like that, about that? Savage, isn't it [sadly]? I was savage [smiles]. I still have that, I know that I did it . . . and I know, *know*, I can still do it [smiles]. (E.P.)

Through literature or film most of us experience a filtered parallel universe that allows only what we want to and are prepared to see. It gives those of us who want it a transient and safe identification with the person using a weapon against an enemy without us having to inhale the stink of death. Audiences for hard contact sport, in general, seek and cherish *duende*, not just in the afternoon but also with physical damage close enough to death. Boxing, in particular the knockout punch, comes closest to showing us death. It is real, not acted, and its meaning often transcends the bounds of the physical.

THE LUSTFUL EYE

> [Combat] absorbs us utterly, it is as though the human being became one great eye. The eye is lustful because it requires the novel, the unusual, the spectacular. It cannot satiate itself on the familiar, the routine, the everyday.
>
> —J. Glenn Gray, The Warriors: *Reflections on Men in Battle*

Killing the man who would kill you while escaping injury is electrifying. Soldiers in contact with the enemy become enthralled. They risk death focusing only on destroying the enemy. The reflex to defend against mortal harm results in lust and freedom—no thought, only action. Winning has completeness. Some men, more predisposed to embracing risk, become intoxicated with it. Our shared drives, which are "the essence of life itself," often become destructive. Joseph Campbell surmises that we all possess, in differing degrees, a tendency to plunder, which is not derived from "biological urgency but of an impulse launched from the eyes, not to consume, but to possess" (Campbell 1956). There are physiologic systems that reward behaviors that ensure individual survival. These reward systems deliver pleasurable responses, such as, for example, looking at the object of sexual desire—even without consummation. "Looking," as an end in itself, avoids the anxiety that accompanies the painful anticipation of rejection by the sexually desired object. Both looking and taking by force deprive the person who is the object of the right to say no. In war, there is always looking without being seen, as through a gun sight, or a submarine periscope.

Nazi propaganda presented the German soldier's eye as projecting, not receiving: "Shining eyes are the prerogative of the German soldier" (Theweleit 1989, 2:135). The eye feasts in war, is engaged by war's constant novelty. Poet Ezra Pound called it "a love of slaughter." In Andalusia, the eye is like a sexual organ and Andalusians prize the *mirada fuerte*—the strong gaze. In southern Spain, rape can be ocular (J. Alonso, personal communication). The Bible speaks of "the lust of the eyes" (1 John 2:16). Marines call it "eye-fucking"—to seek targets and vicariously project killing force (Broyles 1984, p. 56). They get hard doing it.

A photograph of himself in-country reminds E.P., the Vietnam veteran, of what he was and what he had, and he wants it again, like youth, like the absolute certainty felt in the clutch of passion—something precious. In the photograph, he is dark from the sun and from the blackening that happens in combat—from dirt, from the eclipsing of any attention to himself because of the focus on killing. He has, he says, the "look of a killer." He is lean, taut, "bad," and he has no expression. Instead he has "it," he says. "It's right there, in my face." His eyes are exactly the prescribed two fingers below the brim of the "DI cover" (hat) and they are expressionless as they stare into the camera. But what this fifty-year-old man sees in the photograph of himself at age twenty-one is quiet menace. He says,

"Those eyes say 'I have no business with you; you leave me alone. But fuck with me, and I will fuck you up more than you could ever imagine.'"

An eyewitness newspaper reporter to the genocidal revolution in Rwanda described "the wild-eyed young men . . . waving clubs . . . and looking for someone to kill." Groups of Rwandan refugees fear the person, also displaced, whose eyes proclaim his lust, his love of slaughter: "He has the killer in the eye" (Rosenblat 1994).

ATROCITY

Who is the victim, who is the slayer? Speak.

—*Bhagavad-gita*

Little distinguishes the aggressor from the bystander in the Vietnam War. Soldiers on patrol or on reconnaissance in territory that was never fully secured often fired their weapons at any perceived threat. With time, use of weapons was decreasingly circumscribed by official rules of engagement. There were four hundred separate instances of atrocities reported in fifteen years of American presence. Soldiers at My Lai reported they obeyed their orders: "[It was] a search and destroy mission, we were to kill everything . . . Kill everyone . . . Kill everything that moves" (Bilton and Sim 1992, p. 99).

In a novel borne from experience, Tim O'Brien writes about the rural hamlet the U.S. military maps designated as "Pinkville"—My Lai. It is impossible to know from the text whether he was present, but O'Brien writes a scorching four pages. It begins with Lieutenant Calley saying, "Kill 'Nam . . . He pointed his weapon at the earth and burned twenty quick rounds . . . Grease the place . . . Kill it" (O'Brien 1994, p. 105). During the killing of civilians, of old people, of mothers and children, soldiers reloaded their weapons unhurriedly while eating candy bars, lost in their individual and communal evil."[3] One veteran says: "The second time I went back [to Vietnam] it wasn't for flag or country; it was for the killing. It's [pause] addictive" (D.K.). His face changes when he talks of the "killing"—his eyes flash in wonder. An audience watching this on videotape invariably responds with an audible gasp.

What happens as the tether slips loose? The mastery of others in war, the control exerted by the lethal weapon, destroys the humanity of the soldier as well as those the weapon dominates. A veteran says:

I got a photograph, I'm holding two heads—standing there holding two heads by their hair. Can you believe it? Well, there were other guys walking around with heads on poles—like savages, like long ago . . . and nothing un-normal about it, that's the un-normal part—it was normal, real, it was accepted. They took a picture of me. That's how I remember it because of the photo. That's why I still have it—reminds me of those times—without the picture I won't believe it in peacetime . . . In 'Nam you always got something to do, ambush, clean out a VC [Vietcong] tunnel . . . you do it so you can get out, get food, get water, and maybe, but you don't want to think of it, you [will] get back home, back to the "real world." But now you are in hell and you act it. You don't dare think of home, no way. If you try to get home, you worry about trying to save yourself, you get dead. So nothing matters.

The VC I killed . . . Jesus! Well, you had to do it. You had to do it to get out of there. I didn't care about the VC—they would have killed me. But the women and kids? First I was picking them [children] up after the gunships shot up a ville. Then I capped them too. They'd grow up to kill you—maybe that was the story. But that's crazy—but like I said, crazy was normal there. Unless you accepted that as normal, you could not live through it. (N.S.)

Such killers were attached to their buddies, to whom they are loyal:

They would do things, then its over, and you go on. Hell, they [VC] would do it to you, you have to do it to them a hundred times harder and worse . . . So these guys found these women in a village and they started to rape them. Yeh, and they are banging away, and then they take out their K-bars, for God's sake! And they are stabbing them, crazy, out of control, and banging away—crazy—and still doing it when the women are dead.

You understand? Maybe you understand . . . but it isn't possible to get people to understand who were not there. It was terrible what I—we did—but we all did it, those good guys I knew. All good, do anything for you. I can say it, I loved them . . . But the worst thing I can say about myself is that while I was there I was so alive. I loved it the way you can like an adrenaline high, the way you can love your friends, your tight buddies. So unreal and the realest thing that ever happened. Un-fucking-imaginable. And maybe the worst thing for me now is living in peacetime without a possibility of that

high again. I hate what the high was about, but I loved the high. And life in peace fucking kills me with dullness.

God, I went so far down after I came back to this real world, I used whatever I could
to get the feeling back. Booze, drugs or shot some guys, got in real trouble. I couldn't
live any other way, you see? After that speed of things going off all at once, that trust of
those guys, that absolute trust, loyalty—yeh, love. The only way to get some of it back
is to live high on drugs or to get high on some of the danger or to remember what happened . . . You know I wasn't always like that. Can you imagine what it's like to live like
me? (N.S.)

That experience colors such soldiers like a mordant. They are fixed, forever
guilty and ashamed in a way that differs from before they became soldiers. They
are unafraid of terrible things, but fearful of the sweet, the easy.

Atrocities committed and witnessed led to the most enduring and dysfunctional symptoms of posttraumatic stress disorder. In peacetime, with the return
to the "normal world," veterans experienced guilt and "flashbacks."

The Vietnam War had become the permanent part of the peacetime landscape
for a forty-four-year-old veteran who enlisted at age seventeen: "I think I went
to fight communism . . . I was scared all the time, tried to be like the older
[twenty-year-old] guys. They did things, buying kids, using them, raping them,
not caring . . . I can't get it out of my head; I couldn't stop them . . . They shot
farmers in the field, just working, just for—I don't know—just because they could
do it. I was on a carrier with twin .50s [guns], they did it and told me to do it. I
did it, I did it. It was OK at first; I belonged because I was like them. I can't stand
myself for it now" (A.D.).

Some combatants say that killing became amusement and then, still worse,
habit. Soldiers surrounded by a hostile or potentially hostile population lost respect for life and for the individual. Their emotional center shifted to the ability
to kill, to "fuck up" an enemy whose intent was to do the same to them. Some
sought that excitement. They speak of it as "getting away from you," going crazy
with the "power and the killing," the mixture of sexual excitement and relief from
the deadly fear of the killed enemy who would have killed them. They supported
one another in killing and were sometimes supported by a leadership that had
also lost its way and substituted body counts for purpose (Sheehan 1988).

In his comment on the lack of limits in war, Clausewitz (1984) states that escalation is reciprocal and moves toward the utmost exertion of forces. Combatants, ordinary men to start, say that they became killers without noticing the descent into darkness. Ceding individual responsibility to the group and loosening restraint are what made soldiering and war possible, but when command loosens civilized restraint, atrocity is likely.

What is the constellation of forces overriding the restraining force of civilization?

Men at war experience intense excitement—orgasm pushed up a notch, an automatic weapon on "rock and roll." In its momentum toward absolute force, war can engage some of its participants in savage amusement—which defines the perverse—including using other people as entertainment in situations that demonstrate the greatest disparity in power and control.

In Kuwait, during the Iraqi occupation, a story was circulated about a Kuwaiti man who was driving his car with his one-year-old son, when he was stopped by an armed Iraqi soldier. The Iraqi told the man that he had "much power over him": he could make the man happy by being nice to his son or he could make him sad by shooting his son. "What do you want me to do, Kuwaiti. Make you happy or sad?" The panicked man stammered, "Happy," to which the Iraqi reportedly said, "No, today I think I will make you sad" and shot the baby in the head (Saathof 1995, p. 176). Soldiers' matter-of-fact conversation informs us of the ease with which they can become insentient to anything but the excitement of use of force.[4] After soldiers become acquainted with war, such events still shock—but do not surprise. Before World War II, a group of German and Lithuanian men volunteered for and were recruited into the *Ordnungspolizei*— *Orpo*—the Order Police. Their mission was to kill Jews and, with such sanction, these ordinary men carried out the largest numbers of murders of Jews in Poland during the Holocaust. The Reserve Police Battalion 101, a group of middle-aged or older men who had the choice to avoid such duty, became avid professional killers. They enjoyed it and exceeded the expectations of their commanders (Browning 1992). This has occurred over the centuries in the Balkans. Muslims and Christians on opposite sides perpetrated reciprocal massive atrocities— authorized and sanctified. National religious leaders echoed military command and lent moral or theological support to rape and killing.

CONSCIENCE AND ABSOLUTION

Taking the soldiers' oath, I freed myself of the consequences for what I do. I'll do what they tell me and nobody can blame me . . . [Killing without responsibility] seemed a bit unnatural, but for many, not unpleasant. All too quickly it could become a habit.

—J. Glenn Gray, *The Warriors: Reflections on Men in Battle*

In Vietnam: "Before we shipped out of Parris Island, the chaplain gave us absolution, a general absolution. I guessed it was for what we were going to do. I guess that meant to us, to me, that we could do anything, you know all the laws were lifted, we were forgiven, beforehand—wow! . . . They told us about the military code, but we were also told that 'anything goes in-country.' No ifs." (E.P.)

Indeed, soldiers remain troubled about "getting off on it" at the same time that they feel continued excitement in memory.

M.B.: We almost wanted them to fire so we could fire back. I carried an M-16, I had a grenade launcher and a .45 automatic [smiles]. You would be in and out in seconds, seconds . . . free fire zones . . . you could shoot anything that moved. The power was enormous, enormous. I killed somebody—I think I did.

Dr.: How did you feel?

M.B.: I'm afraid that I liked it [desperate]. What the hell is the matter with me? (M.B., former Vietnam medic, now a nurse)

Some are troubled because they feel no remorse: "What is the matter with me?" is a cry of soldiers throughout the history of civilization. A decorated English infantry officer in World War I said that "killing never bothered him"; he later registered his lack of reaction as "failure to suffer . . . shock . . . [and] recognized some deficiency in his own character . . . or, . . . regrettably in human nature itself" (Keegan 1976, p. 25).

Others, used to the ability and reflex of killing when angered, cannot think of peace. "Everyone likes peace but me," said a Serbian sniper, anxious because his war threatened to end. "All I know how to do is kill . . . I can talk to people, but if someone pushes me, I will kill them" (Barnes 1994).

A former Marine in Vietnam seemed impervious to the death he caused; he thought only about "the kill."

Dr.: What is there about combat you like?

B.: All is happening in microseconds, but slo-mo, you're rolling, coming up on target, rounds all around you, whistling, and you want to take them out. That's all you have in your mind, you want that kill. . . . A kill at two klicks [kilometers], that is beautiful [smiles]. It stays with you.

Dr.: Did you enjoy it?

B: Not the right word, more like satisfying—the bullet vaporizes the guy, explodes into him. Satisfying . . . hitting the target—beautiful . . .

Dr.: Could I learn to like it?

B: No. You? You worry . . . about people, you would feel the hole you make. Well, maybe you could be a soldier—but not one like me.

He did not want to be disagreeable and diminish his doctor, but we both knew that he knew the attributes for a combat soldier and the more stringent ones for a Marine. He could see that I could not measure up to either.

REPRISE

Only one of these Vietnam veterans describes himself as having been aggressive before Vietnam, and he has reconsidered his life and disavows the importance placed on that. After returning from the war, only some of these former combatants engaged in physically aggressive activity and have conscious thoughts about killing if provoked. They think about how they would kill in situations if it were necessary. With few exceptions, they are as likely to avoid killing another person as they were before combat. The excitement of killing is only in revisited memory.

Good soldiers do not start out as takers of life; they kill because they must. They are attached to their fellows, to some of their commanders, and to the purpose of the nation and because of that, essential to it, they try not to shirk from killing the enemy.

Much of the psychological damage many veterans suffer can be ascribed to a general human predisposition (with differing individual tendencies) to respond with intense attachment to the killing experience. Susceptible soldiers, once "primed" by the exposure to extreme danger seek more danger in the ordinary peacetime world. Many remain terribly troubled by their continuing attachment to savage satisfaction. Untethered mortal combat can turn us toward our own darkness, to the part of the self that desires destruction. In its finality, the world becomes a burnt offering. This did not happen only in the murky past; it is with us today.

Do we wear civilized clothing on top of armor? A constant refrain here is that the influence of the civilization developing over millennia has become a constant strong force restraining us from human beginnings as "dawn warriors" (Bigelow 1969).[5]

Civilization is restraint and included in all of its regulations is the concern for spilling any blood, not only that of kindred. Civilization extends concern beyond those who are blood relatives to an ultimate concern for all (Tillich 1977) and restrains actions accordingly. In a developed society, regulations and laws shape thought, feeling, and behavior. Civilization provides a reduction and an escape from fixed repertoires of behavior. Our minds are social and develop to as great a degree under the influence of our civilization as by instincts developed as evolutionary adaptations imposed on brains by genetic blueprints. Not only do we save those who are kindred from death but social expectations of action often overcome innate reflexes—even those for survival.

Young men in Vietnam, as in other wars, let loose of the tether, were warned that they must attend to rules that restrained their killing power. Their lives and those of friends could be lost in such restraint, and war offered the compelling opportunity to share with other men the satisfactions of raw power. Many continue to live with guilt because memories of killing are still accompanied by gratification.

PART III
THE TRAUMA OF WAR

FIVE

COUNTERFORCE
FACING TERROR

The terror of war burns into memory.

In the film *Thanh's War* (Farnsworth 1990), a Vietnamese man who grew up during the war and has lived in the United States since 1975, says, "[My childhood] . . . nothing good about it. I wish there were a pill to take so I could take away my story, my history."

In my office, the following exchange took place:

Dr.: If there was some way of taking away the memory of the war, just erase it, take it away leaving no memory—would you want it?

D.K. (former combat Marine, forty-eight years old, now dead): No.

Dr.: And you don't even hesitate. You were in-country for eighteen months and that war imposed [emotional burdens] on you which you tell me made it impossible to live a decent peacetime life since you returned.

D.K.: And I don't care. People say if they had their life to live over—hell, I wouldn't change a thing! It is me, and what I got from it, what I still get from the memory—that is worth it.

Both men felt the terror of the war and long remembered the constant possibility of death or worse. The Vietnamese boy, now a man, and the former U.S. Marine suffered similar symptoms caused by the same war. This chapter examines the difference between the experience of the boy, who wishes he could forget the war, and the experience of the man, who tenaciously held on to combat memories. That difference is relevant to a wider understanding of how all traumatic events are experienced.

Allow yourself to imagine war as a Vietnamese child or as an American soldier. Thanh suffered the war without any power of his own or any expectation that his parents would be able to protect him because they were equally powerless and fearful. D.K. went to Vietnam with comrades, all well equipped to protect themselves and each other. That difference shapes both the subjective experience in situations of stress and contest and the memory of that experience.

Without the real or perceived possibility of effective action to counter the assault against them, humans are forced into the same emotional state that we see in laboratory animals confronted with inescapable punishment. Both are overwhelmed and can become automatons. Devoid of the essential human characteristic of action, there is disregard for self-preservation. In contrast, the capacity for effective action is the prerequisite for the electric excitement humans experience during extreme risk or mortal danger. That pleasurable experience is a reward that may be "wired in," perhaps by our biological and social evolution. It is felt most strongly in victory, in mortal contest.

The person who faces probable death but can reverse that fate by exerting effective counterforce against assault becomes a hero. He has subordinated the force that would dominate him along with all those to whom he is attached. Heroism is a quintessential human aspiration and one that ennobles, indeed makes the person a higher form of human in the eyes of those on his side. His enemies will derogate the very act as strongly as his side extols his heroism. The person who accepts surrender or death without struggle is a victim, only sometimes accorded martyrdom or even sainthood, but not considered a hero.

Victory in mortal encounter is interwoven in memory with the fear and shock of seeing comrades dead and mutilated. D.K. felt the terror of annihilation as did Thanh, but the child, now grown, never had the exultant experience of successful counteraction and therefore remembers and still feels only past terror.

War damages all: children, civilians, and armed soldiers. The combatant who knows that he has the ability to triumph in a deadly fight remembers the victory with satisfaction and joy but struggles with the pace of peacetime life. He is disabled in peace partly because he is not able to give up memories of war's wonder and of a contest survived.

Those who have lived through combat describe an exultation never to be felt afterward. Combat has all of the aspects of the "optimal experience," the most intense high, a moment-by-moment sharply focused involvement. If there is nothing to replace the experience and nothing like it to be found in peace, some former combatants are imbued with the sense of deep and perpetual loss. Many repeatedly and consciously stimulate memories of the positive aspects of combat that sundered their lives and left them psychologically damaged. Some veterans also consciously place themselves in physical danger to reengage the ghost of the past "high." Like D.K., they reject, without hesitation, the hypothetical offer of buying a rewarding peacetime life at the cost of erasing such wartime memories.

People remember winning in any competition, and memories of such an event can temporarily relieve despondency and anomie. It is a part of being human; it is particularly (but hardly exclusively) a part of being male. It is expected and discovered in many situations at war and in peace. Physical contests of any sort can produce it in varying degrees. Triumph, the pinnacle of emotion, is akin to joy. For those who have experienced such feelings, there is, almost invariably, a longing for its repetition. Those who were never in combat can reexperience triumph in the memory of the day they hit a home run, made the catch, or fought and won the game.

Combat is the ultimate zero-sum game. All soldiers know that they can be overwhelmed and killed. Even while they are gripped by fear, they are enthralled and excited by the possibility of winning. Waiting for contact is excruciating. However, the "rush" that comes with engagement triggers a hyperaroused, excited emotional state.

Soldiers try to avoid fearful memories, but memories attached to mastery, to triumphing over the enemy, are treasured, refreshed, and often enlarged. Memories of triumph are interwoven with those of numbing fear and loss of friends and are not always successfully teased out. So memories of the elation of past victory often bring along those associated feelings of fear and loss. The veteran attempts to lose those portions of memory that fill him with despondency, but only some memories of triumph come unadorned. He also wants to keep memories of the dead friends who shared the experiences with him, who protected him as he did them. Afterward, the former soldier may own the certainty that he is alive because he and his friends have met the extreme test: they are alive; their enemy is dead. Even when decades have passed, the memory raises a compelling, satisfying excitement, which can be played against doubt and anxiety.

For the returned combat veteran, the positive attachment to victory found in mortal risk often constitutes a major part of impaired social functioning. Peacetime life pales against war, making it impossible to follow ordinary rules. In contrast, those who experienced total helplessness in attack are left with only the continuing negative, nightmarish affect and decreased self-regard. Thanh, the child in Vietnam, remembers the war with continuing deep anxiety and depletion of spirit, as opposed to the returned combatant, who has similar nightmares of being overwhelmed but remembers triumph and ascendancy as well.

The rules of social encounter, particularly with women, are very frustrating for some men returning from combat. These rules differ greatly from those well learned in war. Peacetime resurrects a vulnerability known by boys before they found war's particular form of manhood in Vietnam, Iraq, on Guadalcanal, in the Ardennes, at Agincourt, or in front of Troy.

The long-lasting psychological effects of war and catastrophes have been documented at least from the beginning of the twentieth century. Spurred by the painful psychological consequences of World War I, Freud described helplessness as the essential precipitant for psychic trauma. Freud also believed that the repetition of events, by review in memory and in actual replication of situations that could lead to the trauma, is an unconscious attempt to master the overwhelming experience of the unassimilated past. His idea adumbrated more current views.

The fulsome moment before the soldier kills anticipates the next instant. It is action at its highest level because it is in extreme contrast to the person about to be voided by force: "his death is upon him, but not dead" (Shakespeare, *Anthony and Cleopatra*, act 4, scene 15, line 10). The soldier who kills an enemy feels at that instant the inordinate satisfaction of destroying his potential destroyer.

Despite the toll of war, a nation or civilization cannot continue to exist without an organized physical force that can be directed against others who would destroy it. No matter how culturally advanced the nation may be, it must rely on its citizens' ability to be aroused to defend against enemies. But that necessary wartime resource carries its own aftereffects for the combatants. After a war, many veterans counter peacetime feelings of vulnerability and restriction with memories of their successful use of counterforce in combat.

In Vietnam, there was greater possibility of effective counterforce against the enemy than in World War I. United States forces were mobile and supported by enormous fire. For soldiers, moments that remain in memory and lead to longing for reiteration fill the need for unrelenting excitement. There also remains the persistent memory of helplessness against a lesser-armed but often more determined enemy. The soldiers from World War I, Iraq, and Vietnam would recognize in each other the similarities of shared terror.

In Vietnam, as in Iraq and Afghanistan, no front divided enemy combatants. Although the American troops were surrounded by the enemy and overrun at times by larger forces who knew the terrain and could melt away, they could bring down enormous firepower on an enemy whose ordnance was principally mortars and rockets. Platoons of Americans could be pinned down in ambush or by a massive enemy onslaught and forced into a passive position, but it was not continuous. American soldiers moved out on patrol, covered great distances by helicopter, went into enemy territory to "pacify" the population, and had practically limitless weaponry. Individual American soldiers could call in apocalyptic air strikes against those from whom they were receiving, or even thought they were receiving, enemy fire (Walzer 1992). Soldiers told me that they sometimes called in air strikes to relieve the tension of waiting during the Vietnam War.

COUNTERFORCE AND VENGEANCE

That gall of anger that swarms like smoke inside of a man's heart
and becomes a thing sweeter to him by far than the dripping of honey.
—Homer (translated by O. Lattimore), *Iliad*

On a spectrum of being caught in a situation of extreme stress, there are two poles—the potential for being overwhelmed and the potential for avoiding being overwhelmed by exerting effective counterforce. Is there a general explanation for reenactment found in those who have been rendered helpless and in those able to act effectively against threatening force?

The pursuit of vengeance feels right and certain at the moment. Those in the thrall of vengeance reject a need, in many situations, for laws. Betrayal, basic wrong, loss of comrades call up powerful forces for retribution against evil. Urgency and the foretaste of satisfaction are savored before the trigger is squeezed or the trap sprung. Courts of law, however, are slow, equivocal, consider both sides, and refer to precedent and judgment on the basis of objectifiable evidence. Regulations and rules of war impose specific conditions on retribution and satisfaction. Law is the pillar of civilization as we know it, and secular civilized societies explicitly reject revenge—*savage* justice. War imposes a different view on civilized people. Satisfaction and justice are found in a trigger pull, and actions are determined by instant reflex; indeed, thinking gets you killed.

Vengeance is intimate with both love and war, and the highest drama of human life swirls around revenge. Grand opera uses the theme repeatedly; it is a constant in popular literature and film. Portrayal of a clear and severe wrong committed, followed by the tables turned, satisfies audiences whose only connection to the specific dramatic events may be some past injustice and victimization. The man about to be killed, who at that moment can reverse the absolute of a predicted zero-sum result, becomes the stuff of heroic legend. Feeling overwhelmed, accepting death and the surrender to it, can yield martyrdom or sainthood but not heroism.

For the soldier, the drive toward vengeance is inevitable and, for many, irresistible. The death of friends stirs anger before underlying grief is felt. Soldiers reflexively give up their own lives just to redeem their friends' lives; the pull toward vengeance overcomes all other needs. It completely possesses and creates an appetite for plentiful death.

In *The Iliad*, Achilles, on seeing the corpse of Patroclus, shouts, "You talk of food? / I have no taste for food—what I really crave is slaughter and blood and the choking groans of men" (Homer 1990, 19:254–55). Geronimo, the Apache chief, wrote from jail to his broken nation about fighting a larger force of the Mexican Army: "the joy of battle, victory and vengeance . . . I could not bring back the dead Apaches, but I could rejoice in this vengeance" (Daly and Wilson 1988).

Indeed, the depth of vengeful motive can be seen in Robert G. L. Waite's description of combat experience in the Freebooters, the German Freikorps. "The turmoil of our feelings was called forth by rage, alcohol and the thirst for blood. As we advanced heavily but irresistably toward the enemy lines, I was boiling over with a fury that gripped me—it gripped us all—in an inexplicable way! The overpowering desire to kill gave me wings. Rage squeezed bitter tears from my eyes . . . only the spell of primaeval instinct remained" (Waite 1952, p. 23).

From Vietnam: "They got one of ours—you want fifty of theirs . . . [You become] drunk but conscious . . . like just wrapped up in the moment . . . a hot needle in the brain . . . just wanting to fuck them up. You moved out into a ville, took some fire, kept going, killed VC [Vietcong] and you're back at base. I'm here and alive and those that are dead, well they're gone . . . Like you lose connectedness because you only want to hurt them [VC] back and you begin to want only the killing. Sometimes you forget why. It has a life of its own, its own satisfaction, the killing does" (N.S.).

The taste for revenge is so strong that it resists any respite in the level of the contest and even prefers that suffering continue undiminished, so that the enemy can be more severely savaged. In those still strong, injury endured contains anticipation of honeyed revenge.

In the middle of the Battle of Britain in World War II, Winston Churchill declared in a broadcast speech to the British public: "We ask no favor of the enemy. [If the people of London were asked whether a convention for bombing all cities should be agreed on,] the overwhelming majority would cry, 'No, we will mete out to the Germans the measure, and more than the measure, that they have meted out to us'" (Churchill 1941).

Many American soldiers extended their tours of duty in Vietnam to get back at the enemy and discovered that the killing can be addictive. The pleasure of vengeance, however, does not deliver the contentment of usual happiness; rather it is more like delirium, an altered state of mind, as if drugged while in sexual embrace.

COUNTERFORCE AND MEMORY

Victims of overwhelming trauma often try to relive the experience of the assault that harmed them. Those who have been raped by an overpowering assailant, overrun in combat or hurt by natural disaster reiterate the disaster in dreams, in fantasy, and often in real reenactments. Experiencing again the most damaging event in our past runs counter to the expected avoidance of painful memories. The wish to savor victory again "turning the tables" on an attacker is more easily understood.

Survivors of such assault sadly confess that they seek out situations that have a high probability of assault—a repetition of the "nightmare they lived through." One woman, raped as an adolescent, repeatedly walked in dangerous areas late at night and was attacked again. Such patients often say that they find themselves in such dangerous areas without memory of planning and that they feel "addicted" to the behavior but cannot explain it. One veteran (R.O.), referring to memories of Vietnam, said, "they give me a kind of little high . . . Vietnam hooked me, the way a drug would." Some also put themselves at serious physical risk in dangerous situations, but with concomitant satisfaction and pleasure, which former soldiers know, but which resists civilian description. Only afterward do they wonder why they look for trouble. Yet in danger, there is some momentary calm; they feel reassured and satisfied, but such risk demands repetition. A forty-five-year-old former combatant who became a priest because of what he witnessed in war, reflects, "You know, I think I am nuts, really. After a late meeting in church downtown, I will walk across Boston Common sometimes at midnight. It's for the high of danger . . . I can't stop, it's like an addiction . . . I got it in Vietnam. I want to be rid of it. I want all of us [veterans] to be rid of it. I want all of us to be at peace, in peace" (O.T.).

Unlike drug addicts seeking a high, these veterans have no conscious anticipation of pleasurable excitement. After surviving such a sad revisiting, they feel, as one woman said, "terrible, dirtied" (F.M.). They want to stop recapitulating their sad past. Does a person reenact memories of being terrified and overwhelmed and yet intensely want to avoid the repetition of terror? The repetition of trauma by seeking places where attack is highly probable has been the subject of conjecture and theory, both from a psychological viewpoint and, more recently, from neurobiology research on the addictive properties of neurochemicals, endorphins, and opium-like substances found within the brain and released under stress (Pitman 1989; van der Kolk 1989). The neurochemical view of addiction to trauma also includes the role of dopamine, another potent neurochemical. The neurobiologic description of what we would see as the attachment to or addiction to past traumatic events is uncertain. For the trauma victim, there is a tendency to maintain a personal view of oneself as a victim, a strong characterization that crowds out the perception of other attributes.

Most of us have the potential for attachment to victimhood. Victim identification enables people to have the emotional support and strength that accompanies belonging to and identifying with a group of fellow sufferers. Such feelings have political consequences. Those who have experienced a history of ethnic oppression, for example, African Americans in America and Jews in the Holocaust, identify with each other as victims of brutal oppressors who denied their humanity. After the war, Germans took on the mantle of victimhood, describing themselves as victims of their own propensities for single-minded duty (*Pflicht*), which carried them insensibly to war and to oppress others. They were, then, liberated by the victory of the Allied Forces, as were other Europeans, including the Jews. Some expressed the sense of liberation as did other Europeans. The position of victim can be pernicious even though it is manifestly understandable. It is often difficult for victims to find joy in survival, in endurance, and in the accomplishment of being part of humanity (Sleeper 1997).

Victims of trauma who had no means of effective counterforce hold dormant memories, unpredictably restimulated in dreams and flashbacks; sometimes the memories are acted on in a dissociated state of mind, which has the appearance of a volitional act. Soldiers who "relive" stressful events in which they were able to use effective counterforce report feelings of pleasure and satisfaction.

A past experience of grave threat overcome by active counterforce eases the memory of terror once felt, sweetens the experience enough to make for pleasurable repetition, and renews the sense of potency and mastery. Victory is followed by release, by a "rush," a "high." While all of us have felt that in varying degrees, those who know battle have experienced it in the highest degree; they have triumphed over the real possibility of death. They have vanquished the enemy who would kill them.

Combat veterans describe trying to selectively "tease out" in memory those aspects of the experience in which they can anticipate and reexperience a sense of control and mastery in the face of threat. If events of triumph are too close to those of loss and terror, the combined memory is avoided. With such stimulation, either by physical action in dangerous situations or by retrieving memories, they temporarily escape alienation, apathy, and the feeling of loss of valued purpose, activities, and persons.

Victory entrains excitement, satisfaction, and release of tension. This is further informed from animal studies: the opportunity to attack effectively is behavior that is, in itself, rewarding. The potential for turning the tables is high drama; athletic victory against the odds captures headlines. Audiences in theaters and movies relive such triumphs. We can't get enough of it.

Historical and literary narratives over the centuries report and celebrate the triumph over danger and defeat universally and in so many contexts that it cannot be assigned to individual psychopathology. A severely stressful situation that still permits effective counteraction colors the emotion attached to the experience and the memory in which the experience resides. The appropriate use of aggression in such conditions facilitates attention, thought, and behavior rather than helpless immobility. It is probably associated, as well, with activating different brain reward systems "wired" to deliver feelings of satisfaction and pleasure in response to such specific stimulation.

ACTING ON AND ACTED UPON

There is a vital difference between acting and being acted on. Animals exposed to inescapable shock in a laboratory exhibit symptoms similar to those of humans traumatized in war or overwhelmed in threatening situations: abuse of young children, rape by a powerful attacker, the Holocaust, and natural disasters leave emotional scars on people.

Yet the most intense and prolonged stressful situations, which all of us would judge to be traumatic, often allow the person attacked to "do something," some opportunity to either escape or overcome danger. Only some human experiences are comparably as overwhelming as that contrived for the unfortunate animal locked in a cage on a charged grid from which there is no escape. That outcome is only sometimes realizable, and it is usually impossible to assess the potential for effective action at the critical time of assault.

For humans, there is dismal meaning attached to the failure to act. It lessens and often shames us. A missed opportunity for effective counteraggression troubles us usually with a feeling that we should have acted differently: "if only I had . . . " Boys grow up schooled in the idea that we should not yield in the face of danger; honor is accorded to those who actively defend themselves, who "fight the good fight." The ability to respond effectively depends on individual and group ability to use available force. A former combatant makes a clear distinction: "Oh, yes—we are in our holes, and every night they [VC] started mortar attacks—shit all around— they were yelling and we were scared—that's what comes back to me and wakes me up—sweating, heart pounding—couldn't take it. But a firefight? Yes scared, but going like hell, pumped up, high. It could last for seconds, maybe minutes—it was a lifetime. I think I loved it; afraid I loved it. I know that I dwell on it a lot and cannot let it go although it has nothing to do with the living here and now" (E.P.).

People who have been traumatized by overwhelming force try to solve their own problems by ruminating thoughts, dreams, and activities to find a way to "make it come out right," to vindicate themselves through more effective action. They accept the impossibility of the task only slowly. Very often, such victims of trauma try to master that which cannot be mastered. A melancholy and dark emotional coloring accompanies these attempts at mastery and therefore contrasts with conscious memories of those former combatants in Vietnam who have told me of the vivid experience of severe threat connected to effective counteraggression. Soldiers find it satisfying to reiterate past experience in active combat; they try to avoid memories of situations in which they were forced into a passive state of intense terror. Victory following helpless terror tends to nullify the painful aspect of the memory however. The terror may come back as unwanted, intrusive flashbacks and dreams, but the veterans do not try to reevoke it, focusing instead on the memories of effective counterforce. Combat gives moments of transcendence through effective counterforce as well as horror.

We can view psychologically traumatic events within a spectrum. Anchoring one end are those situations exemplified by the rat in a laboratory setting controlled so that effective counterresponse to danger is impossible. At the opposite end are situations in which effective counteraggression is a real possibility, such as waiting in a prepared ambush armed with effective force. Both kinds of situations generate tension and stress but one imposes an anticipation of being overwhelmed; the other bears the anticipation of success. One person is demeaned by the prospect of being turned into an object; the other anticipates transcendence from the ordinary and exultation in victory.

That particular need of human beings to be the active participant, the "operant" person rather than the "respondent" has moved great forces in history. Such forces are reflected at the most elementary level in animal physiology and reflected in many arenas of human life. Those of us who play competitive sports know of the difference in feeling after even a small triumph, even in those who deny it and claim to be playing only for the "exercise." The winner feels better than the loser; the aging athlete who wins feels less muscle and joint soreness. People play to win and also play to re-experience the high that comes with winning. Athletes who are behind in a game but finally win it chronicle the memory, reciting the seeming inevitability of defeat followed by the unexpected victory. It also is true for onlookers. If "your" team wins, there is a greater sense of certainty, well being, and exhilaration, matched by the despondency in the supporters of the other team. After a match, testosterone levels mirror such changes. Levels are higher in the winners and lower in the losers, for fans watching and cheering their teams as well as for participants.

All psychologically traumatized people try to grab hold of psychological control and effectiveness after severe stress and damage. The fact of survival after being so close to death leads to a reflexive response to regain control. The difference in being overwhelmed as opposed to being successful in using countering force affects how people pursue memory and enhance fantasy. Those who have been overwhelmed, hurt, and subordinated wherein they lacked any ability to change their status, often desperately try to regain control by repeating and revising the event in dreams, fantasies, or reenactments. They attempt to experience a state other than the deplorable feeling of powerlessness; they repeat the experience to achieve mastery, *this time*. They desperately and sadly seek a sense of control over a past, uncontrollable force.

The need for control over opposing force is only human, necessary for self-respect and apparent in *all* attempts to restore control and to master traumatic situations. That tendency may be "factory installed" in us, part of our evolutionary shaping toward dominance and fitness, a necessary survival mechanism for coping with adversity. When men fail the test or anticipate failure in mastery, they become anxious. Anxiety, often termed the "human condition," is the personal experience of "there is something I should be doing now that I am not doing"; depression is experienced as "it is too late now to do anything." Amid a firefight, fear banishes anxiety, combatants are forced to concentrate on the most demanding and immediate—mortal danger. In war, men are judged and judge themselves by values that differ from those by which most of us are raised. Moral judgment is directed toward consequences: that which helps survival of self and friends is good. Intent is of no consequence. "The test" has the promise of erasing male anxiety forever. It may do that, which is a part of the attraction of war. Men's self-esteem has been strongly shaped by evolutionary and cultural pressures toward use of counterforce rather than surrender. Amid the gravest danger, adaptation and survival have been served by the exhilaration of successfully repulsing force with force. Failing to do so, even if the possibility of successful response to overwhelming force to save oneself or a comrade is slim or nonexistent, is psychologically devastating, and the memory is haunting. The man so burdened will carry the damage, and people around him also will be likely to suffer. Men die rather than accede to failure; women, too, feel the human need to avoid subordination and, similarly, attempt to regain mastery after overwhelming trauma.

CHAPTER

SIX

DAMAGE

WAR'S AWFUL AFTERMATH

You hear the sounds of wounded men after the firefight. They can't be quiet, they are shouting, crying out for help—indescribable but I can still hear it in my head. There are bits and pieces of friends, and all the pieces are crying.

—R.M.

By the end of the World War I, there were thirty thousand reported psychological casualties, and by 1922, there were fifty thousand. The number of British soldiers seriously psychologically affected was probably far greater than reported (Winter 1979). But that war exacted proportionately fewer emotional casualties in Great Britain than we would expect today from our experience in Vietnam.

The difference in psychological casualties in a war is often said to be influenced by the degree of a nation's popular support for the war and its goal. As dreadful as World War I was, it was regarded, like World War II, as possessing good purpose. Shared purpose eases the psychological wounds of war. Civilians during the Battle of Britain generally rallied together in shared loss and suffering. As a consequence, there was a less than expected level of acute psychological damage from bombing and even a decrease of the usual "neurotic symptoms," such as psychosomatic disease and minor depressions causing dysfunction.

The Vietnam War killed fifty-eight thousand Americans and three million Asians. The psychological effects on combatants are still being tallied decades after the withdrawal from Saigon. All wars exact a profound toll of physical and psychological damage. But what is the nature of this psychological damage?

Many veterans seek to reduce the symptoms of the psychological trauma caused by war's terrors. At the same time, these men often have a continuing positive attachment to the very war that sundered their lives. This is because war, with its closeness to mutilated bodies and atrocity, creates an unyielding necessity for continuous hyperalertness. The fear aroused occurs in tandem with the other aspect of war that the combatant finds so compelling: intense bonding with "brothers," the magic of weapons, the use of force, and revenge—the enemy who would kill you, now "dead in the dirt."

At least 50 percent of America's Vietnam combat veterans are still burdened with varying degrees of psychological distress resulting from the intense stress of combat (Keane, Zimering, and Caddell 1985). One estimate placed the number of veterans dying prematurely after returning home at two times the number killed in the war (Capps 1991), and a high proportion of those deaths are related to psychological problems brought back from the war. Exposure to heavy combat (Bremmer et al. 1992) and especially to atrocity (Green et al. 1990) is a major factor in the frequency of psychological and psychiatric disturbances in Vietnam veterans. To that can be added the strain of fighting a war far from home in unfamiliar and inhospitable surroundings.

POSTTRAUMATIC STRESS DISORDER

Specific symptoms resulting from war experience are commonly referred to as "posttraumatic stress disorder" (PTSD), a designation in psychiatric nomenclature that emerged largely from clinical experience during and after the Vietnam and subsequent wars. According to diagnostic criteria, "The person has been exposed to a traumatic event . . . in which the person experienced or witnessed or was confronted with an event or events that involved actual or threatened death or serious injury, or a threat to the physical integrity of self or others, responded to with intense fear, helplessness or horror." The characteristic symptoms resulting from traumatic exposure include persistent, intrusive reexperiencing of the traumatic event through flashbacks and recurrent dreams with persistent avoidance of stimuli associated with the trauma, numbing of general responsiveness, and persistent symptoms of increased arousal. There is intense psychological and physical distress at exposure to external cues and thoughts that symbolize or resemble an aspect of the traumatic event (American Psychiatric Association 2000, DSM-IV 309.89).

As suggested in the definition above, PTSD starts with an extreme psychological trauma. The victim is helpless, driven into passivity by overwhelming force. In combat, there is the constant presence of the enemy, the awareness of the probability of death increased by the inevitable viewing of mutilated bodies. Soldiers are repeatedly drilled to respond with counterforce, to go forward "toward enemy fire." Combat trainers repeatedly shout at them that they must not "hunker down"; if they fail to return fire, they will certainly die. Worse still, they will have failed their brothers. Soldiers go into battle trained, with weapons, and with the multiplied strength of their comrades. With that and high morale—confidence that they will dominate—they will turn the tables on the enemy. Combat soldiers' PTSD derives from the constant terror that they will not win (always a possibility), that the enemy will prevail, and that they and their friends will die. They may have been overrun by the enemy and barely survived. They view mutilation constantly. All of this evokes a sense of powerlessness and leads later to symptoms of trauma. The traumatized soldier lives in a continuing state of high alert in peacetime. Danger is sensed constantly. A car backfires or a firecracker explodes and he reflexively dives to the ground. He sleeps fitfully, wary of attack, reliving moments of acute anxiety and panic.

Returned veterans with PTSD attempt to avoid situations that might prompt unexpected "flashbacks," the unwanted, intrusive revisualization of memories of sudden unexpected mortal threat. They continue to re-experience the moment of terror when the surprise attack rendered their response ineffective. They live with the still felt possibility of being forced to take the effect of overwhelming, annihilating force passively. A man fighting with a past enemy wakes up in his own bed and realizes that he is strangling his wife.

Back home, some veterans "hole up" during the Fourth of July because they have experienced reiterations of attack with the sights and sounds of fireworks. The noise of a helicopter overhead, explosions, and smells, all can spark a massive reaction. Flashbacks leap out unpredictably, shoving aside reality, shattering rational thought. Past terror still colors dreams and makes sleep fitful. Very few veterans sleep well, and some carry around a perpetual dark shadow of guilt over their savage satisfactions.

At the same time, veterans with PTSD knowingly, repetitively, and selectively stimulate memories related to mastery over the enemy who was trying to kill them. Those memories afford a temporary pleasurable arousal, but they also trail behind them the attached memories of horror. Veterans who were in the trenches lived in a position of passive endurance in close proximity with those who shared their experience. Veterans remember that endurance and bonding with comrades were the major determinants of their survival of that war.

With time, however, the aging Vietnam veteran, still locked into youthful experience, inevitably and sadly realizes that his attachment to memories is a yearning for the unrecoverable. Now, more than thirty years later, some of these men in their fifties and sixties have also concluded that seeking the hot memories of war contributes to a chaotic and unrewarding existence. Some avoid talking about the war, even with other veterans in group therapy: "I know they are supposed to help, but these groups just get me wired up, guys bragging, all of us getting high on it—then I leave and feel lousy, because there is no place to take it" (R.O.). The "high" found in the group is temporary, and they are left with the enduring knowledge that dead comrades are forever lost, and there is little in present life to replace what they had in the months of war.

For many, a constant dark shadow of guilt about the satisfaction of and charge in killing in successful counterforce lingers:

A crew chief and gunner on a Huey (widely used military helicopter) registers the excitement. He suffered a stroke eight years after his return, causing increasing difficulty with language and comprehension. He speaks of Vietnam with intensity; his facial expressions are best described as tortured as he struggles to make himself understood. At times, his meaning is very clear. He concentrates hard as he laboriously writes in block letters: "KILL V.C. WIFES, CHILDREN ME." He points to himself and imitates the action of the machine gunner and the sound of the 60 mm weapon. He painstakingly draws a picture of the gunship with lines showing its trajectory, writing "SLOW." He puts down the pen, imitates the gunner again, then writes, "50 + KILL. ME." He now has a look of excitement.

"Did you like it? Exciting?" I ask.

He smiles suddenly, brightly and nods; then, immediately after, his face takes on an expression of such despair that I become concerned.

"It bothers you that you liked it?" I say.

He says, "Why?" Then writes: "KILLING ASIANS. LOST EVERYTHING. 7 CRASHES. DEAD. (points to himself) NOW ME."

"You died—you're dead?" I respond.

He nods vigorous assent. (C.I.)

Another part of the damage inflicted by the Vietnam War came from its lack of coherent goals and the inability of those in charge to articulate clearly a just purpose and an end to the war. As our longest war ground on and body counts replaced any goals, the soldiers knew that they were not moving toward defeat of the enemy, although they were able and willing; the political process interfered. In Vietnam, the combatants felt that their effort and the deaths of brothers were in vain. V. D. Hanson writes that "G.I.s in World War II were killed in pursuit of victory, not [as in Vietnam] in order to avoid defeat or pressure totalitarian governments" (Hanson 2001). He might have added: or to avoid a political debacle for the president.

Although war, in Clausewitz's terms, "is different from anything else" (1984, p. 55), it pales in comparison to the ordinary sorrows of the rest of the soldier's life. All former combatants carry some part of the war with them, although not all have the full array of symptoms; they have degrees of distress and anxiety, hyperalertness, inability to sleep, and persistent emotional volatility. American veterans of World War II who had only some symptoms suggestive of PTSD died younger than did a similar group of men who had not gone to war. Peacetime relationships are damaged by PTSD symptoms and are often aggravated by the use of alcohol and other drugs.

The responses of traumatized people are part of a normal coping process that helps them get through stressful situations. Hyperalertness is appropriately adaptive: high levels of alertness aid survival in combat. You cannot be too alert as you face an enemy who would kill you. But, when the soldier leaves the war, he may continue to be hyperalert; the threat is gone, but the psychological response to mortal threat remains as a behavior pattern, diminishing good functioning in peacetime. His unceasing wariness and denial of fear, a necessity for combat functioning, severely limits human relationships in peacetime, which is a major persistent dysfunction after traumatic stress.[1]

Traumatologists who investigated the origin and effects of trauma in the past few decades have emphasized "real" events occurring in any environment as the origin of posttraumatic symptoms. The contemporary view endorsed by most professional therapists is that psychological stress inflicts damage as would a "series of blows" (Terr 1991). Judith Herman describes trauma as an "affliction of the powerless" in which "the victim is rendered helpless by overpowering force" (Herman 1991). Any allusion to a predisposition to symptoms of trauma from any source has been perceived as "blaming the victim" and was avoided in early work on PTSD, although recent work defines certain attributes that may predispose some people more than others to symptoms.

The best model for PTSD attributes it to uncontrollable, overwhelming force that imposes a helpless and passive position on a person (Keane, Zimering, and Caddell 1995). Animal research that measures physiological changes paralleled by behavioral responses shows that punishing stresses from which there is no possible escape causes an animal to become passive and helpless, curling up in a corner, whining, defecating, and urinating (Krystal et al. 1992). The animal looks as if it has given up; they develop learning deficits, inattention, decreased motivation, and apparent persistent distress. The experience of stress permanently changes them. They continue to act strangely, indeed "neurotically" or "psychotically," and make no active attempts to escape. Our understanding of the traumatic effects of war on humans is greatly enhanced by these studies.

Guy Sajer, a German infantryman in World War II, was deafened by the intensity of the noise that followed a white flash. The air around him was sucked away and he was buried under the earth: "Trapped by the weight of the earth, I began to howl like a madman . . . The sense that one has been buried alive is horrible beyond the powers of ordinary language . . . At that moment, I suddenly understood the meaning of all the cries and shrieks I had heard on every battlefield." This soldier continued to live fearfully with that memory forty years after the war (Sajer 1967, pp. 327–328).

Not every combat experience inflicts traumatic aftereffects. The threat or anticipation of death alone is not powerful enough to initiate continuing psychological symptoms (Yehuda and McFarlane 1995). Symptoms of PTSD in soldiers are related to the exposure to sudden death and bodily mutilation—seeing it and especially smelling blood or the stink of death "close up and actual." There is reason to believe that smell is the strongest stimulus to recognition and memory;

perhaps it is an evolutionary legacy when the sense of smell was more important to humans than it is now. A Vietnam veteran recalls arriving on the site of a past ambush—"the smell, oh God, the smell" (R.M.). Most, if not all, veteran combatants speak of the stink of war that remains in their nostrils. The smell of dead bodies, so unforgettably unlike any other—the "stink burned into the brain," says Vietnam veteran D.K.

Constant exposure to such experiences dramatically destabilizes the belief in the predictability of the world; that is why war is like nothing else. Those severe combat experiences are "indigestible," not assimilable. The returned soldier has them in memory, and they are further reiterated as flashbacks, their intensity unchanged decades after the assault.

ASSAULT: THE PHYSICAL DAMAGE

Many kinds of assault are experienced in combat. There is the constant fear of death, the possibility that an enemy by superior force or surprise can pin down or overrun a platoon. Soldiers who were trained to return fire while moving toward the enemy, rather than responding to the reflexive impulse to hunker down, experienced greater helplessness. There were inevitable attacks in which troops were immobilized and unable to return effective fire. Those who survive such helplessness suffer from intrusive memories of those events. It is every combatant's nightmare—and for some, that image comes back years after combat to disturb sleep and purpose.

Marines just arriving in-country learned about death right away:

We came up to Danang, a long ride—in a truck—we had no weapons yet, and we were plenty scared.

We get there and we are told to start loading body bags. You have to lift the bodies, see, and slide them in—and sometimes the bag opens up and you're pushing the body or parts of the body of some American soldier back into it with your chest or chin . . . and the knowing that it could, would be me that some other FNG [new recruit] would be loading next week. (R.M.)

The soldier seasoned by combat tends to the wounded and the dead with the greatest concern. Because friends and self are so fused in battle, caring for friends—even those who are dead—is tantamount to taking care of oneself. Some veterans can speak now of the emotional aspect of taking care of comrades, wounded and dead, in a controlled, distanced manner. Fred Downs, author and former Marine lieutenant in Vietnam, said:

> It's difficult, you know, when a guy is blown to pieces and say he's still alive and his leg is blown off. You pick up the leg with your bare hands and carry it . . . You don't even look at the leg. Most guys can't do it. They'll take it and keep their eyes averted and put it on the stretcher . . . You get right down to tying off the stump, you've got to do that but looking at the severed limb or when your [i.e., their] brains are blown out, that's a thought that always stays with me. One of the men got hit on one of the patrols and the bullet clipped the top of his skull and it just opened up like a melon and the brain went all over. It's such a strange feeling to see that, and then you have to collect it up as much as you can and put it all together in a pot or helmet or whatever.
>
> Dr. N.: You do that despite the continued danger to the living while under attack?
>
> Mr. D.: Well, you don't leave a body or parts behind. That's an obligation we feel for each other. It's very strong. (Fred Downs, personal communication)

Another veteran tells of staring with great interest, for too long a time, at a single, intact index finger lying on the earth without mark or blood—like an unfamiliar, newly formed alien creature. That image is fixed in his memory, both obscuring and standing for all the other horrors he had witnessed.

The damage their weapons could exact on enemy soldiers not only filled unseasoned soldiers with terror but also with wonder and excitement: "You have to see the hole you make, the black hole in a chest, blacker than anything, deeper than you could know. Some guys would go up and look at it close, poke at it. Then some would smile. Jesus, it made me wonder . . . and some guys couldn't take it, we couldn't believe the kind of damage we could do" (E.B.).

Another veteran talks of the aftermath of a firefight, the sudden sobriety when the wild intoxication of contact abruptly ends and the calls from the wounded and dying are heard. "You know what you hear? They are all crying, 'Ma!, Ma!' They can't stop—crying, 'Ma!, Ma!' Jeez, Marines wanting their mother . . . You want to tell them to shut the fuck up! Jeez, I was afraid that I would do the same thing. Those cries are still in my head. I hear them now in any quiet room" (E.P.).

On the Eastern Front in World War II, the German infantryman Sajer faced two captured Russians. "The two wretched victims . . . kept imploring his mercy but Lindberg, another infantryman, in a paroxysm of uncontrollable rage kept fir-

ing until they were quiet . . . We were mad with harassment and exhaustion . . .
We were forbidden to take prisoners . . . We knew that the Russians didn't take
any . . . For me, these memories produced a loss of physical sensation, almost as
if my personality had split . . . as I knew that such things don't happen to young
men who have led normal lives" (Sajer 1967, p. 186). He described the memory
of the carnage of battle—pieces of bodies, viscera plastered against walls and tree
stumps, the ground saturated with blood, a vista of corpses with a smell so nau-
seating that it "stays in the nostrils forever" (Sajer 1967).

Soldiers who lose themselves in the grim satisfaction of revenge often feel
guilty afterward. The death and mutilation of one's comrades engender great an-
guish and savage anger at the enemy soldiers who killed them. Wild with rage,
soldiers wish only to sate their revenge, sometimes even killing those who are
weaponless and have surrendered. They do not regard the soldiers they kill as
like themselves.

In World War I, "Reid once emptied three Lewis gun drums into a German
platoon, with fierce satisfaction at doing the frightful execution at Morval" (Winter 1979, p. 133). Afterward he saw a dead German soldier holding a crucifix in
his sole remaining hand. He and his comrades were shocked and contrite; they
had not expected the enemy to die like themselves (Winter 1979, p. 133). At Passchendaele, a New Zealander, after a fierce and successful attack on a German position, hardly noticed the limp bodies of the German dead until he found himself
looking at a young, mortally wounded German soldier. Moved to tears, he gave
him water and put a cigarette to his lips (Macdonald 1988).

A sixty-six-year-old World War II veteran (W.B.) sought psychiatric treatment
in 1985 for anxiety accompanied by an obvious tic, a sudden, sharp turning of his
head to the right that began soon after his return. He spoke to me of his experience for the first time:

> So we've been up through the islands, lots of contact . . . I'm a sergeant, twenty-four,
> getting old [smiles], I'm thinking of home, my wife and the kid.
>
> . . . I'm on a point [leading his platoon] with a B.A.R. [Browning automatic rifle].
> And the war is winding down, I only want to go home . . .
>
> We're just mopping up . . . and then this Jap, a kid maybe like me, he comes out of
> the bushes, scares me. I turn and let him have it—I just open up and kill him. So, then,
> like some damn hero, I fish the body. Jesus, why did I do that? [Anguished, he passes

his hand over his face.] And he doesn't carry nothing, not even a jackknife on him, just a wallet. There are pictures of his wife and kid ... [weeps with rapid movement of head to right] and [shouts] that's the son of a bitch who's still bothering me" [continued movement of head]. The tic gradually disappeared after six visits in which he repeated more details of the event.

FRIENDLY FIRE

Men die in wars not only through error in judgment, lack of information, or accident but also because of blunders stemming from their leaders' incompetence. A lack of faith in the command's ability to make strategic decisions and to protect soldiers erodes morale and weakens soldiers' cohesion with the leaders. That also damages the survivors.

During World War I, British soldiers at the Western Front recognized that many comrades died because of their leaders' inability to assess situations and their failure to use greater firepower against a better-armed force. At the War's beginning, the British soldiers knew that they were outgunned by German artillery (Winter 1979), but British leaders believed in the superiority of the English rifleman and his Enfield, perhaps a carryover of the romantic view of the superiority of the English archers at Agincourt. Hard-eyed critics of these commanders documented the stupidities of leaders who, although often revered, were at times dilatory or out of touch and failed to press their advantage when they could or made "side shows" for their own advancement without regard for strategy or the lives of the men at the front (Dixon 1976). T. E. Lawrence wrote that "the men were often gallant fighters but their generals as often gave away in stupidity what they had gained in ignorance" (Fergueson 1999). To conceal his failure at Neuve Chappelle in 1915 and enormous losses of troops in repeated attacks, British general Sir John French blamed a lack of artillery shells (in fact, there was adequate ordnance). The government, in turn, blamed the munitions workers and enacted regulations to restrict the open hours of public houses, imposing an afternoon pub closing that was amended only in 1987 (Taylor 1966).

"Friendly fire" and other unintended combat tragedies have killed soldiers in all wars. The soldier under attack can know only his narrow sector. Soldiers fire on those who seem to be trying to kill them; some of that fire, in every war, is misdirected toward friends. In the Gulf War, Afghanistan, or Iraq, U.S. casualties from friendly fire were often greater than those imposed by enemy forces. War always has friction, missteps, miscalculations, delays, incompetence (Clausewitz 1984). Some disasters, in retrospect, could have been avoided by careful planning and communication by command. A poorly planned "rehearsal" for the D-Day landing ended in the drowning of many allied soldiers before they could face enemy fire. Operation COBRA, a misdirected bombing on July 24–25, 1944, intended to help U.S. troops break out at the St. Lo beachhead, killed 135 Americans and wounded more than six hundred (Fussell 1989). Such events were widely known among troops at the time, although civilians were shielded from such news on the grounds of "military security." The effect on the soldiers is mistrust of command and a suspicion or even conviction that command used the troops capriciously and without concern. Decreased morale also leaves residual mistrust as a part of the dysfunctional symptoms of posttraumatic disorder.

Effective competence of commanders and their concern for their soldiers strongly bind command and soldier. When soldiers are victimized by incompetence, the loss of trust and faith they experience on the ground persists, for many, at war's end and contributes to the meaninglessness felt in peacetime by those with posttraumatic stress disorder. War may have had some coherent purpose at its outset, but that purpose is often lost on the combatant. Meaning and purpose are reconstructed at war's end, largely to appease the public, when the country celebrates the sacrifices of its returned soldiers at parades.

Wars that last too long often lose their meaning for the soldiers fighting in them. They are mortally endangered, and they often say that they lose any idea of why they are fighting. They have "lost their bearings." They are "just trying to get home." These soldiers are often not in contact with their task and are probably at greater risk of being killed. Beyond specific damages, war shakes soldiers loose from the meanings we ordinarily attach to other people, and its heat evaporates preconceptions of what is expectable. The loss of meaning is central to the emotional damage of war veterans bring home.

MEANINGLESSNESS

World War I was celebrated on the medals awarded to the British soldiers who participated in what was termed: "the Great War for Civilisation, 1914–1919."

In Pat Barker's novel, *The Ghost Road,* the poet Wilfred Owen hears a fellow officer state that the war was "feathering the nests of profiteers" and another say that
"we are fighting for the legitimate interests of our own country . . . for Belgian
neutrality . . . for French independence." Owen says that the war has no reason,
nobody is in control, and nobody can make it stop. The theory that it continues
because someone is profiting is also optimistic and just as romantic a notion as
that the war is for Britain, Belgium, or France. For the soldier, in Owen's words,
there is only the immediate, the stumbling in the dark. In answer to patriotic fer-
vor about the innate savagery of the Germans, Owen says: "You say we kill the
Beast . . . I say we fight because men lost their bearings in the night" (Barker 1996,
p. 144). If war was constructed to kill the enemy as a beast, then the soldier in
combat fights only to get out of it alive with his friends.

War is inherently traumatic because it dehumanizes its participants. The soldier loses meaning, that is, a sense of purpose, goals to strive for, principles (such
as respect for life) to protect. The soldier cannot afford to give weight to anything
outside of the immediate, which is to survive. Made helpless by the enemy or by
loss of faith in command, he is exposed to an assault on the senses by continuous terror, carnage, mutilation, guilt, and the stink of the battlefield. Leadership
that is inept or arrogant also magnifies soldiers' distrust and strains and breaks
the loyalty to that which gave his life meaning before the war. The soldier is angry
with leaders who have no connection to the narrow perimeter of his war. He is
angry with the officers on the ground who use up soldiers' lives in blind obedience to orders, by caprice, or for ulterior motives.[2]

In Vietnam, many combat officers provided leadership that elicited deep loyalty from their troops; many others, however, were not up to the task. Incompetence or lack of personal courage compounded the soldiers' sense of betrayal
from the war's incoherence and their lack of connection to its cause. Soldiers dis-
connected from any purpose, save their own survival, openly expressed anger at
betrayal, even to the point of "fragging," or killing their officers for revenge and
to save their own lives.

Many soldiers were damaged by a sense of betrayal: they went to Vietnam to
protect the United States, but as the war continued, recognizable benefit to the
United States was lost. When the soldiers returned from Vietnam, a grateful nation did not thank them. The returned veterans were surprised to find themselves
ignored or hated because of the war. Soldiers, especially those of democratic na-

tions, do not have an enduring blind trust (Hanson 2001). The purpose of war matters much to the soldiers who fight it. Combatants back from Southeast Asia were returned abruptly to "normal life" without cleansing rituals and without any communal understanding of what had happened to them. Interest in the Vietnam War trailed off, and the nation and its leadership, ambivalent at best about the War, did not organize parades and memorials until a decade later. As the War slid to an end, there were no rituals of expiation for the soldiers, no parades to close out their time of killing, to welcome them back to a world of expectable rules, of relations between people. The public disavowal of the War and the soldiers' sacrifice also intensified and perpetuated the symptoms of war stress for many veterans.

All severely traumatic experiences damage the moral sensibility; war demeans all participants by its nature. That is, it removes dignity and drives soldiers to unimaginable actions in peace. It "demeans" in that it decreases the human meaning of "normal" loss; it demeans as it burns away the usual attachment to respectable meaning—the quality and value of actions and persons—and replaces it with the imperative of survival alone. The existential dilemma pondered by adolescents and philosophers about life's meaning dies in combat. That which was imposed as necessary, the rules that society provides to support meaning for life beyond simply "being," are killed by combat's capriciousness.

As children we are taught that there are differing consequences and judgments for "good" as opposed to "bad" actions; and moral effort is defined by understanding the degrees between them. We are also taught that conformity to those principles leads to reliable expectations that life is, on the whole, predictable and fair. That is our civil foundation and also defines the ideal of what is human in peacetime.

War is far more aleatory, unpredictable. Death "just happens"; there is "nothing to be made of it." The constant urgency and unpredictability of war make it difficult to assimilate the meaning of loss, even when a friend is killed. A friend is suddenly dead, without warning: "He had just turned toward me, and in midstep, I saw something take away half his face—his face chopped in half like by an axe" (O.T.). In combat, the meaning of loss does not register because of the soldier's overwhelming need to stay alive. Anger and the urgent need for revenge become the quickest cover for grief.

The returned combatant often suffers from a feeling of "nothingness." Life in combat held intensity and, in that, an undefined but vivid meaning. The soldier obeyed the nation's command; that command set him apart from the rules. In war, higher purpose with expectable rewards is ground to dust for some veterans. A familiar phrase used by soldiers in Vietnam is "nothing happened." One participant self-protectively summarized a firefight in which close comrades were killed as "it didn't mean nothing." Such attempts to negate attachments are only partly successful; repeated experiences of such loss turn meaninglessness into an enduring, reflexive habit. In this negation of meaning and moral responsibility, there is a dreadful freedom, which is not transportable out of combat. Life in combat is remembered by some as one remembers a delirium—some parts absolutely clear, others unassimilable.

Those rotating out of Vietnam, dirty, ragged, tired, and "used up" saw, as they were leaving, the fresh troops, the FNGs, coming into country. The veterans, as they passed the new guys, called them "meat," partly from combat-learned cruelty, indifference, and disdain but also out of the recognition that the FNGs were innocent and were now stepping into the unimagined. The constant probability of death and its unpredictability for the individual may initiate a "numbing of feeling" that is an important symptom of posttraumatic stress. One veteran at age fifty went to his daughter's wedding and invited a fellow veteran with whom he has a close relationship. Reflective and full of wonder, he was disbelieving at watching his daughter's friends dance:

> They were beautiful, happy, just dancing. We could see that they were living a life we did not have, so free and loving. We can't dance—if we once could, we can't now—can't loosen our bodies for it. But it was the easy loving feeling toward everybody—I think that was what made us uncomfortable, we couldn't share it. They came over, smiling and respectful and we managed to keep them from talking to us by our expressions and lack of response, we just nodded, heads down. We couldn't look at them—couldn't look at love. What could we fucking say anyway? All I could think of was that if someone hurt them, we would hurt those people back, but all we can ever bring to the table is fucking violence—that war. It is all we are now. (E.P.)

It is in the nature of war that soldiers must commit mortal acts that etch their lives in ways that they or their families never could have forecast. Vietnam may be written off as an adventure of lost purpose for those in charge. That would make it an absurdity—history's worst judgment—remembered only as a cautionary tale. But there is more to every war to be remembered—the suffering and death on both sides and the sacrifices it exacted from soldiers. Our soldiers were caught up in war's horror and wonder; they were intoxicated by it, wounded, killed, but not responsible for it. It is the nation's responsibility; the loss of meaning would not have been the soldiers' burden if we had not sent them away. It is fair to say that these men might have had problems in living even had they not gone to war—everyone does. War, however, imposed the unexpected for which they could not have been prepared. These veterans continue to suffer from war's terrors but also from the nothingness that came from their indoctrination into violence. Vietnam also damaged us—it is the end of our belief that we always act justly, fairly, and kindly. It is the end of our innocence. We can kill unjustly, and we will again.

For many returned veterans, the heroic myths of fabled wars erode under the onslaught of visions of exploding bodies, of carnage, and of devastation. Strive as they might to retain the "echoes and re-echoes" of duty, honor, and country, the many sorry souls who cannot are doomed to remember an eternity of war's horror. Labeling the outcome "posttraumatic stress disorder" virtually trivializes a consuming experience.

Sadly, we must repeatedly go to war, and we will put men and women and the nation at risk. It is best that we understand that using force by sending soldiers into "harm's way," where they may experience "intoxicating freedom" in the midst of mortal danger, includes the real danger of our soldiers losing moral stability and values learned as children; as a nation, we risk no less. The risk is greater if we do not pursue this with determination and intelligence and our leaders' clear statement of purpose.

CHAPTER SEVEN

MYTHS AND PERCEPTIONS

The ordinary kids, raised on John Wayne and soldier heroes, believed that a war that was so extraordinary would make *them* extraordinary also—the sanction and ability to kill was intoxicating in the doing and in the promise of respect thereafter: "You could do anything you wanted—shit, I was eighteen—kill anyone or anything in Vietnam and get away with it. It was like being drunk and walking around with a hard-on" (R.M.). Soldiers returned from war who have experienced the loss of war's wonder suffer from degrees of sadness, or anomie, a state of lassitude and lack of social connectedness, often resulting in anxiety in sweet peacetime.

Another veteran said: "I got up in the morning after sentry duty and felt that warm sun, stretched in it. I'd give anything for that feeling right now. I was in it, with it, I could see all that was going on . . . Like I went through something to get [that feeling]. I've torn loose from ropes or whatever . . . Not afraid of anything, not worried about how I was doing, how I looked—if I died, so I died . . . [sadly] I came back and they wrapped around me again; it hurts more now because I had that . . . With my people, the excitement, the constant highs. I can't have it again. Fuck this [peacetime] world" (D.K.).

Before the reality and awful aftermath of actual battle, mythical preconceptions of the glories and agonies of war were gleaned most compellingly through movies and literature. Literature, including representations in various media, shapes our memory of wars we lived through, even sometimes for those who were combat soldiers. War is larger than life, so different from anything else, the courage and sacrifice of soldiers so vivid that their actions merge with fiction and give war's memory enduring reality. Literature about war becomes the war remembered. The literature we create shapes us in return, often more than does historical fact. The wish to create myth usually outruns truth, and lies are seen as necessary to create heroes. Although some say that without heroes we would perish, it may also be argued that we have wars to create heroes.

We humans have the unique capacity through language to make symbols with meanings that grow more compelling over time. And we respond to such symbols, the products of our own making, more than to fact, indeed, as more important than anything else, including our lives. We have gone to war for family, home, country, flag, blood, dignity and self-respect, roots, the queen, or empire. We make savage war for civilization. Such human constructions lead to war if intensely felt symbols are threatened. This was strikingly true in fascism, where the people of the nation were forcefully presented with a vision of their true ancestral characteristics. Movements like fascism offered a return, a *palingenesis,* to the identical images from the past, creating a mythic rebirth and regeneration often tied to the annihilation of their enemies (Payne 1995). But that phenomenon is not solely confined to fascism.

The parallel universe of myth and story about war has a more enduring hold on our consciousness than the reality, and this is also true for combatants who were in the war. Myth shadows and becomes the reality and is remembered afterward as truth. War movies, even those intended to be realistic, are accepted as real only when they reflect back to us our desired fantasies of war. If we didn't have war movies, we would be left with the terrible truth of the reality of war.

All literature is perhaps a dissent against nature, a reaction against its indifference to us, and in that, a prideful assertion of our unique humanity, an insistence that what we do and suffer has greater meaning than reality often allows. All writing about any subject is fiction in the sense that writing is not it, but *about* it, even scholarly histories, eyewitness accounts, or recorded video or film. Although this idea may seem extreme, the multiplicity of perceptions of particularly dramatic events such as war is impossible to present in any one document. Any single document or observation of war acts like a lens, filtering out some aspects, intensifying others, and representing the war from an observer's point of view. The war of civilians, of commanders, of officers at headquarters, of those removed from the stained edge of battle, is not the same as the war of the men on the ground. No whole or "true total picture" is possible. Indeed, fictional history—war imagined—sometimes captures the emotional texture of the moment better than an objective record (Fussell 1989; Hynes 1991). Historians and journalists attempt to report events with some congruence to truth, but their work includes the writer's prejudices—a desire to present and embolden a particular aspect of the war most acceptable to the public audience. The need for myth and for larger-than-life heroes often outpaces the truth and has better "legs" for the long run.

Much of what is human resides in our ability to create our own "landscape" of shared myths (Schama 1995). The world we know, the one we assume to be "real," may exist within all of its different descriptions.

War experienced remains a life focus, and although war is not fervently desired by everyone, men become intoxicated by it, certainly at the start, but women less so (although shifting social mores and attitudes suggest that this needs to be reexamined). War literature preserves that, enhances it, tells us of the reach of battle and the reach of love. The literature of war shows us what we can be at our most noble.

LITERATURE FOR WAR

Organized combat first appears in the Hebrew Scriptures in Genesis 14: Abraham organizes an armed force of more than three hundred men in an assault against foreign kings to rescue his son, Lot. The Hebrew Bible's "bardic tradition" elevates warriors to a place of honor and in this regard is similar to the chivalric character of other classics (Niditch 1993).

The literature of war both attests to war's terrors and shapes the chronicle of war into a bittersweet, beautiful adventure. History and fiction have presented war as shared courage, sacrifice, nobility, and comradeship in the midst of the excitement of mortal danger. War as represented in literature is the showcase for the male ideal. Horace exhorted Romans toward an ideal of sacrifice for the empire, but he did not know anything of the painful, dirty, bitter nature of dying in war. His view was at a filtering distance. Time and repetition have further purified and sweetened it. English schoolboys, innocent of war, have repeated his words for centuries.

A war story achieves perpetuity through its ability to stir the heart, not through accuracy. The story of how the name "Tommy Atkins" became synonymous with that of all British soldiers has been retold many times.

In July 1843, a junior officer asked the Duke of Wellington to settle a minor detail of war administration. A name typical of the private British soldier was to be printed on a pay form to indicate where a soldier should sign. The duke remembered his own first action in the Low Countries and a soldier whom he had seen after battle. Thomas Atkins, a twenty-year veteran, had been cut by an enemy saber, bayoneted in the chest, "and had a bullet in his lungs." The bearers tried to move him but he asked them to let him die in peace. Wellington looked down on him and the man must have seen his concern: "'It's all right, Sir,' he gasped, 'It's all in the day's work.' They were his last words." The duke relayed the story of "Thomas Atkins" to the staff officer, and British soldiers have been called "Tommys" in every war since then (Macdonald 1988).

Such myths constitute much of that we know and want in war. They shape our understanding of it and establish war's reality. We desire a commonality of cause and brotherhood with the heroic, which the uncomplaining sacrifice of the soldier to leader and nation can provide. The verity of this desire slips past our critical judgment and can evoke from some men, even against our will, a reflexive tightness in the chest, a cry painfully stifled. When at war, we demand conviction to strength, purpose, and justice, and we want only to be stirred toward love of our own and resolve against the enemy. Winston Churchill, himself a maker of myths, once declared that the truth is so important that it must often be protected by lies. William Blake, a pacifist, believed that classic literature is the strongest force in perpetuating war.

INVOCATIONS

The men who went, often gladly, to the Great War in the last century were sustained in part by a classical educational system that fostered a cult of heroism and patriotism. The grinding horror of World War I was coupled with a prodigious literary output that helped to sustain first the effort to endure and then the memory of that conflict (Fussell 1975).[1] Rupert Brooke expressed the fevered delirium for clash and conflict felt in England: "Now God be thanked who has matched us with His hour." That was before the first great wave of casualty lists came crashing back.

The cadence of classical rhetoric served Winston Churchill in the darkest days of the War. On June 4, 1940, after the Battle of Dunkirk, he summoned up British courage: "We shall not flag or fail. We shall go on to the end, we shall fight in France, we shall fight on the seas and oceans, we shall fight with growing confidence and growing strength in the air, we shall defend our Island, whatever the cost may be, we shall fight on beaches, landing grounds, in the fields and in the streets, and we shall fight in the hills; we shall never surrender, and even if . . . this Island or a large part of it were subjugated and starving, then our Empire beyond the seas . . . would carry on the struggle" (Churchill 1940).

Readers both at home and at the front were eager for reports and poetry about the war. T. S. Eliot, who frequently struggled with the elusiveness of his craft ("Words . . . slip, slide, perish, / Decay with imprecision, will not stay in place"; "Burnt Norton," Eliot 1967, p. 175), nonetheless found an enduring lucid moment in Britain at war. The phrase "History is now and England," from his poem "Little Gidding" (Eliot 1967, p. 197), would actually become a battle cry in World War II (Fenton 1996). Everyone wanted to feel purpose, direction, something other than the intolerable anxiety that came with helplessness and suspense (Hynes 1997).

Skillful writers, who were not soldiers, wove an image of the British soldier for the public. Kipling (1915) dedicated his book *Soldiers Three* to Tommy Atkins. The "Tommy" was idealized in his stoicism, in his stubborn ability to endure; sacrifice became enshrined in such literature. Times of greatest severity seem to hold more truth, seem more real to the participants than quotidian times. That is why war is such a great vessel to hold both myth and literature.

Hear the suggestive, graphic fullness of MacArthur's last threnodic address at West Point—his voice, plangent; its cadence measured by the distant drumbeat of artillery, evokes a fading twilight, softened by the haze of battle smoke. "The shadows are lengthening for me. The twilight is here. My days of old have vanished, tone and tint; they have gone glimmering through the dreams of things that were. Their memory is one of wondrous beauty, watered by tears, and coaxed and caressed by the tears of yesterday . . . In my dreams I hear again the crash of guns . . . the strange, mournful mutter of the battlefield . . . I come back to West Point. Always there echoes and re-echoes in my ears—Duty, Honor, Country" (MacArthur 1962).

MacArthur conjoined battle, sunset, his own fading away, and reshaped war, as many have, into a revered landscape. It is not meant to be analyzed or logically understood but to "reach the depths before it stirs the surface" (Cox 1993), to pull the listener into reverie and to move the heart, to reassure us in our belief in the dignity, purity, and even the beauty of the soldier's mission.

When soldiers returned home, myths were replaced with reality; the world of peace closed in on them. Peacetime made demands—opposite those made in war—that made them angry and resentful at having been primed for war all their young lives and to come back to the sameness, the daily unchanging sameness. Returning soldiers found public disregard or contempt for the war. Family at home did not want to hear about war's terror more than once from their son or brother or daughter. The joy in mutually shared respect between soldiers about war's excitement could not be shared with civilians; its wonder was inarticulable, and much of what veterans could say would not be believed.

"I wanted to come home to my mother but I started drinking, fucking-up anyone who got in my way—because I knew how to do that. I couldn't do the civilian talk—'discussion.' My mother couldn't understand. She knew I was in trouble and looking for more—but didn't understand—how could she? I still loved her like always but what she taught me I couldn't use anymore" (E.P.).

MYTH TO REALITY

In his 1995 book, Robert McNamara, secretary of defense during much of the Vietnam War and the prime artisan of its policies, confessed to knowing early on that the War was lost in irresolution, yet he continued down the same path, yielding to the pressure of policies directed toward the containment of communism. He confessed that he attempted to elicit support for the War at home while knowing that the effort and the consequent deaths were going to be greater than any advantage gained (McNamara and Van de Mark 1995). One book reviewer wrote that, with this book McNamara had "paid his debt," referring to the information owed to the public about the War (Draper 1995). After the former secretary discussed his book in public on national television, however, some veterans expressed raw, unadorned, savage anger toward him in a unified voice. One man cried in rage about a friend lost in Khe Sanh. Many said they wanted time with him alone—they had questions. Few felt compelled by the argument that in misleading Congress, the American people, and the combatants, dead and alive, he had acted only out of the necessity imposed by political pressures. Veterans could not acclaim his courage in self-revelation by setting the record straight. That kind of courage, after the fact of the deaths of comrades, continues to erode the spirit of those who fought what some call "Mac's War" (D.K., R.M.). The book did little to diminish the Vietnam veteran's sense of betrayal.

The irresolute pursuit of the Vietnam War's foundered purpose changed Lewis B. Puller's attitude of unquestioning loyalty to military leadership. Puller, the son of the renowned Major General "Chesty" Puller, the most decorated man in the history of the Marine Corps, changed his views after becoming a casualty and had time to reflect on war's damage. He went to Vietnam as a Marine second lieutenant, and within a week in the bush, tripped a booby-trapped howitzer round: "I thought initially that the loss of my glasses . . . accounted for my blurred vision, and I had no idea that the pink mist which engulfed me had been caused by the vaporization of most of my right and left legs . . . I could see through a haze of pain that my right thumb and little finger were missing, as was most of my left hand . . . I knew that I had finished serving my time in the hell of Vietnam" (Puller 1991).

After returning home, Puller became disillusioned with the War. When the Vietnam Veterans Against the War assembled in Washington, D.C., to protest the War's continuation, he learned that many of his "brothers" in combat now viewed the War and its sacrifices as "meaningless." He considered traveling to Washington to join other veterans in throwing away their medals. But he realized that "they had cost me too dearly, and though I now saw clearly the war in which they were earned was a wasted cause, the medals represented the dignity and caliber of my service and with whom I had served." His ambivalence toward the Corps remained; he was attached to it and despised it (Puller 1991). Lewis Puller lost a run for Congress, but won a battle against alcohol. He died in 1994, before his rightful time.

Another Vietnam veteran, Ninh Bao, a man who fought on the other side, is one of ten surviving members of "the Glorious 27th Youth Brigade." He was in combat against the Americans from 1969 until 1975. His memoir, *The Sorrows of War*, describes his life in combat, its terrors, and the horrendous constancy of terror, deprivation, killing, and mutilation. After the war, he had all of the symptoms of posttraumatic traumatic stress disorder noted among our veterans: he avoided human contact, suffered from intrusive memories and flashbacks, drank constantly, and was unable to form a permanent relationship. For him, life in peace was only a different kind of hell. Like his American opposites, he was disaffected from his government, which he saw as corrupt and insensitive to the veterans. Yet he remembered the war's excitement and comradeship with longing (Ninh 1993).

Philip Caputo returned from combat in Vietnam and became actively involved in the antiwar movement; yet, he still wrote of the nostalgic pull of the War (Caputo 1977). Even those mentally or physically damaged in war continue to both love and hate the War and cannot totally reject it. That feeling, which they cannot and do not want to shake, consumes many of them and has wounded their ability to live as civilians in peace.

A nation gives the soldier the privilege to kill and sends him armed to endure war's privations and dangers. As recorded in the Old Testament and in the histories of most nations, soldiers were given public cleansing of the "defilement of killing" through "the expiatory rituals" of parades and memorials (Niditch 1993). Such events are meant to "end" the war and finally free soldiers from the guilt of killing.

EIGHT

THE WONDER OF WAR

"We're no longer soldiers," Alessandro said quietly. "That was a lifetime ago. Everything has changed."

"Yes," said the proprietor, "but once, a lifetime ago, we were, and sometimes it all comes back and moves my heart."

—Mark Helprin, *A Soldier of the Great War*

War is our secret sharer. Its constancy in our lives and attraction after years of peace are difficult to deny. At times in the past, nations have embraced war as a lover in a state of intoxication. Ordinary men who have been to war remain attached to its arresting elements, to its *wonder*.

Wonder is the changed state of mind caused by an encounter that shifts the usual and expected into something dramatic, dazzling, and bewildering. Wonder happens when an event unexpectedly lifts a corner of the ordinary universe to reveal another plane of existence. For anyone who has been in serious combat, it claims the pivotal reference point for an entire life, and it strangely shadows, eclipses, all that happened before or after.[1] War unites contradictions, destruction and beauty, love and hate; it illuminates and darkens all of world history. Closeup, it simultaneously frightens, repels, fascinates, and sexually excites. Amid loss of the usual boundaries for what is real, soldiers feel a strong, often unshakable bond with friends who come to share a commonality of experience and enduring love (Bradshaw, Ohlde, and Hjorne 1991; Nadelson 1992). War offers endless exotic experiences in exchange for its intrinsic horror.

We should find a "moral equivalent of war," as William James hoped, but nothing will equal its arresting intensity. War is totally engaging and very serious. War presents unequivocal certainty about the intersection of life and death. Life embraces death in war; death sustains and nurtures life in a contradictory coupling that gives to both a new and clearer meaning.

The young have the greatest susceptibility to wonder. "Things happen in a half-second," soldiers say—a friend slumps over dead as you talk to him, an enemy mortar round lifts a soldier off the ground and lands him five feet away, still alive. A veteran says: "I have had enough 'I couldn't fucking believe its' for a lifetime or two" (O.I.). J. Glenn Gray, a writer and combatant in World War II, generalized that "people are often bored with a day that does not offer variety, distraction, threat and insecurity" (Gray 1970). Bill Fowler, a stretcher-bearer in the Ypres salient during World War I, said, "In a way I lived my whole life between the ages of nineteen and twenty-three. Everything that happened after that was almost an anticlimax" (Macdonald 1978, p. xiii). Herr said, after an intense firefight in Vietnam, "And every time, you were so weary afterward, so empty of everything but being alive that you couldn't recall any of it, except to know that it was like something else you felt once before. It remained obscure for a long time, but after enough times the memory took shape and substance and revealed itself . . . It was the feeling you'd had when you were much, much younger and undressing a girl for the first time" (Herr 1991, pp. 135–136).

AN AMAZING FREEDOM

The men I spoke to discovered the freedom that comes with release from restriction on aggression. In the shared and altered state of mind of combat, these soldiers fiercely defended what was immediate, the future too faraway for consideration:

I want to eat, I eat . . . That [can of peaches] is mine, everyone wanted peaches, but they wouldn't try to mess with me . . . I'd fuck them up. What I wanted, I had . . . We [the Marines] were given nothing, no showers or barracks, just dirt. The Air Force—they had everything, cold beer, booze, getting laid . . . but what I had, I owned and no one, no one, would fuck with me . . . We, 'my people,' I call them, could take anyone on . . . We acted crazy, crazy—but the war was crazy—doing crazy things was the sane thing in a crazy place. That was being free. I discovered freedom. I don't have that now, and I miss it—it's terrible how much I miss it. (E.P.)

This former Marine, now more than fifty years old, speaks with heat of his continuing attachment to the wonder of that time and place and how it changed him and hurt him and how he still could never give up the memory of it. Former combatants, including even those with disabling psychological and emotional problems from the war, continue to reflect on their time in combat. They continue to yearn for the high and transcendent experience of completeness, realness, unambiguous and intense bonding with friends, and a feeling of youthful invincibility, shared in war and lost in peace. Soldiers repeatedly speak of rare, pellucid moments in war, of battle's "terrible beauty" (Yeats 1997, p. 183). Their memories include its terrors, but more vivid are the exciting, exultant moments. War is "the greatest game" throughout history. De Lisle, a World War I soldier, "disliked war in principle but the war years were the best of his life. No sport can equal the excitement of war, no other occupation can be half as interesting" (Winter 1979, p. 224). A renowned historian, asked what he felt while World War II was going on, said "'Wonderful,' he said. 'Wonderful'" (Keegan 1976).

There is excruciating hyperalertness in the midst of the boredom of waiting followed by the release into "the ecstasy of contact" (Caputo 1977). In combat, a veteran says, "everything happens in less than a second." The combatant first sweats out the wait for contact, struggling to keep alert against the weight of fatigue and the gentle insistence of sleep. Once in the fight, Michael Herr writes, "[the feeling] came back the same way every time, dreaded and welcome, balls and bowels turning over together, your senses working like strobes, free-falling all the way down to the essences and then flying out again in a rush to focus, . . . reaching in at the point of calm and springing all the joy and all the dread ever known by everyone who ever lived" (Herr 1977, p. 144).

The same response is expressed in the earliest narrative exposition of human history, *The Iliad:* men are "eager" and "yearning" for battle. Indeed, the Greek word for "combat," Knox writes in the "Introduction," shares the same Greek root as the word "rejoice" (Homer 1990).

Those who have lived without touching these extremes of experience may find it difficult to grasp the engaging aspect of war and the continued attachment to it. Police officers, ironworkers who work up high, circus performers, those who also have a life of risk and hard contest know "the pump," the "high," "the adrenaline." They anticipate it, seek it, and want the feeling that astonishes and excites.

Many former combatants attempt to recapture war's wonder in memory; they feel an irresistible pull toward memory of the feeling and reenactment of wartime danger in peace. It gives them a buzz. Some chase the high of mortal danger by seeking physically dangerous situations, the way an addict seeks another hit. Many describe themselves as addicted. The memories of wartime feelings are "fixed," as a photograph is fixed; that is, the image held, but fading with time, is still readable, emotionally evocative. Memories, in the words of one veteran, "give me a kind of little high . . . Vietnam hooked me, the way a drug would" (R.O.). Those who put themselves at serious physical risk feel a satisfaction and pleasure that former soldiers know but that defies usual civilian understanding. Afterward they wonder why they look for trouble. In the danger, there is some momentary calm; they feel reassured and satisfied with the excitement. When the high wears off, they are more available to rational reflection, but soon after there is a need to taste the high again.

Life in combat is immersion with all the aspects of "flow," the "optimal experience," with concentration on the clear goal of survival or revenge, without self-consciousness or awareness of time's passage (Csikszentmihalyi 1991, p. 49). Combatants describe being "in it"; they do not speak about the events of war as having meaning. Life in combat is not "about anything" but simply "is." That simplicity relieves anxiety of fearful encounters.

When the brain reward systems are firing, everything feels right, and there is no need for an external moral sanction; the good feeling speaks only of the rightness of the moment. With your brain buzzed, the feeling of flow, of one's control and certainty amid the unpredictable, sometimes carries a person with it into evil. The worst abominations in history have felt good, just, and rewarding to some of those perpetrating them. Only afterward might there be remorse, when the larger picture of violation of essential civilized rules is recognized: the bonfires at Nuremberg, the phalanx of brown shirts, worshiping the leader and allying with him in a wave of love to subordinate and destroy the pronounced enemy.

War is usually considered a means to an end. For Clausewitz (1984), it was an extension of diplomacy by other means. However, war has very often been considered an end in itself for which there is no real substitute. Only mortal contest gives a man the opportunity to put everything at risk and to test his ultimate worth against an opponent. An important reason we may have wars is that many men simply like fighting.

Robert Waite, writing about Nazism, quotes a member of the Freikorps after the end of World War I. "People told us that the War was over. That made us laugh. We ourselves are the war" (Waite 1952, p. 42).

A Vietnam veteran says:

You get into it, moving like on a checkerboard, ville to ville. Everything clicking (smile). Your weapon is on rock and roll and you are also. Your response is automatic. Nothing bad can happen to you—like you're convinced that the feeling of everything clicking and being together with your people, will keep you all safe. You get back to base and you're with your guys, you're like a big fist together, doesn't matter then what your color or all that other shit. Your guys are your guys and there was this—I can't describe it—this going through the day and everything working, mellow, you know, but so clear, so much attention, so focused that you could react the right way each time—right in a heartbeat. For that minute, safe and together, with your people, safe because you were with your people, living another day—where there was a world out there trying to make you dead. Nothing ever before or after like that magic. (E.P.)

Viewing life and death up close ages a boy but makes life, if only for moments remembered, fulsome and beautiful, full of boys' excitement. These men love the war they remember, and many of those who survive can still summon up the war's exhilaration. As one fifty-year-old Vietnam veteran confessed, "I was never so alive . . . I know I can't get the feeling again. That can make me cry, if I could cry" (R.T.). Another veteran: "I found the war like I was looking for it. I was like a newborn baby . . . It was like a banquet . . . excitement, oh, God . . . with your tight buddies, and, sure, scared to death all the time. Surviving [it] made me what I am. I was nothing before. I cannot think of myself without thinking about Vietnam" (R.M.).

Aging veterans often desperately want to get back to the war. One veteran told me, passionately, sincerely, and drunk, that the only thing he wanted was to get back: "Just have them drop me in the jungle, that's all, now. Otherwise I'll die here—please . . . Why not?" (S.V.). The next day, sober, he said that the wish never went away.

A different Vietnam veteran, Bao Ninh, who fought on the other side, in his novel about the "Glorious 27th Youth Brigade" describes his life in combat, his constant fear of death and mutilation in a landscape colored "by blood." He suffers from symptoms of wartime stress, but he also speaks of being anchored to the excitement of mortal contest and bonding with his comrades. He has the same bitterness felt by some Americans returning home. His return was more clearly in victory, yet also without parades—"no trumpets, . . . no drums" (Ninh 1993).

FEAR OF DEATH ABOLISHED

Yea tho' I walk in the shadow of the Valley of Death, I fear no evil because I am the meanest motherfucker in the valley.

—A Vietnam slogan

The fear of death can fade with constant acquaintance; soldiers find a dreadful freedom from this fear granted by the war that cements continuing attachment to it. Sometimes, intoxicated with a feeling of immunity, inhibitions dangerously disappear. The soldier goes *berserk:* "I took off my shirt, no flak-jacket . . . jumped up at the perimeter, in plain sight and shouted at the VC: 'Do it, do it you bastards . . .' laughing, crying, shouting. Somebody pulled me down and I'm still laughing" (N.S.).[2]

A veteran reflects on an instant in Vietnam:

Mortar rounds . . . I saw the flash then, voom, voom! I was knocked over, arms and legs going all the time like I was swimming, all so fast! But in slo-mo . . . Trying to get back into position to be ready for them again. Shit, I felt high. High! Like nothing in the world could kill me. I'm twirling over and over, and I know I'm not really hurt or dead. No! I'm so alive I couldn't believe it. You can't believe it because it didn't happen to you. I was on the big pump, no drug in the world like that. The world turns around in less than a second . . . I could take on anyone, we, that's us, could take on the whole VC because we felt just then so strong with each other and way beyond fear of death. (E.P.)

His attachment to the wonder of that experience, to its thrill, is still evoked more than thirty years after the event. Peacetime satisfactions pale alongside that memory.

There are, indeed, some men who were in love with war before they felt its embrace; men who sought dangerous excitement early in their lives. As boys, many did not expect to live into old age and seemed to be actively trying not to. A twenty-nine-year-old former Special Forces soldier, cited for bravery in Panama but subsequently severely injured and physically impaired in a fight, recalled his youth: "I would drive my Honda under [moving] trucks on the highway. Even as a kid I never expected to live past thirty maybe. I am surprised [to still be alive] and I don't know if I know how to live quietly for the rest of my life. Such living is, for me, like slow dying" (P.K.).

THE COMBATANT, OTHER MEN, AND STOLEN COURAGE

One World War II veteran claimed that he volunteered repeatedly for combat but was kept behind as an orderly. He reflected on how he spent his war badly. He gambled with other soldiers on payday and successfully managed to avoid most work. At age sixty, he said, with profound regret, that he had really wanted combat, and now he "will never know" (Terkel 1984).

Men who are relieved for being spared combat yearn for it later, not the terror but the high of directed purpose and the bonding. They wish that they *had gone through it, had passed the test.*

Men who have killed, or soldiers who have come close to it, usually are respected and envied by other men, even if they are living unhappy lives. Other men are in awe of soldiers' use of deadly power and are assumed by noncombatants as having passed the "test" of their manhood. Men who have not experienced combat seek familiarity with it by talking to veterans and vicariously sharing their experience. Combat veterans are disdainful of the "wannabes" (R.O.).

Because courage in the face of mortal danger is less common for humankind than avoidance, some soldiers feel forced to steal courage—a self-helping falsehood necessary for their self-esteem. Many veterans enlarge on their exposure to mortal contest, borrow the experiences of others in war, and cut some of the fabric of the combat stories of other men to wear themselves. The fictional actuality they have created, when repeated to eager listeners, can become reality for the audience and the speaker. Men who lie about having been in combat, try to take from it an unearned satisfaction and a shaky reassurance of their own manhood. One veteran saw prurience in that. Those guys, said one veteran, are "Peeping Toms," a term that hints at how sexual excitement is part of the mix of war's horror.

Even if they were not in combat, many men seek some proof that they could have survived combat's test. Many will accept something "close enough" as proof for themselves. They may fill the gaps with a believable fantasy, wanting to live with the conviction that they would be able to do it if necessary. Christopher Isherwood, who grew up in England during World War I, registered this tangle of feelings: "War in [a] . . . neurotic sense meant The Test . . . of courage . . . maturity . . . of sexual prowess: 'Are you really a man?' . . . I longed to be subjected to this test; but I also dreaded failure . . . dreaded failure so much—indeed so certain that I should fail . . . that I denied my longing to be tested altogether" (Holmes 1989, p. 59).

Ian Buruma, who was born in the Netherlands and lived as a child through the German occupation, wondered, if he were an adult during the time of the Germans, would he have had the courage to fight in the Dutch Resistance or would he have betrayed others to save his life? He hoped that he would have been up to the task but knew that he would have been frightened and might have avoided such danger, recognizing that "failure is more typical of the human condition than heroism" (Buruma 1994). Many young men who wrestled with their fear and the moral dilemma during the Vietnam era requested and received psychiatrists' letters indicating unsuitability in order to avoid combat. Those for whom I wrote letters seemed so extremely unstable and anxious that I concluded that they would be more of a detriment than any help to their units. Some came back to see me or other psychiatrists because of misgivings and lingering concerns about having avoided the test.

A former combatant says he knows that he has an "edge" on other men; those who have not been in combat regard him with awe:

E.P.: You know, all the others, even politicians, who weren't in the war, now they want to be with us, with the guys, the 'Marines' who were there. Want to have their pictures taken with us. Talk with us, like pals.

Dr.: What do you think they are after?

E.P.: Well, they want to be like one of us, to have been there, through it. They try to act like us, talk like us . . . Maybe they figure other people will think they are vets also, that they have been through it also. Maybe other people will believe that they are combat vets—and maybe they themselves get to [believe it] also.

Dr.: What does being "through it" mean to them?

E.P.: Well, it means you know something that isn't in books. You *have* something [*because*] . . . You [are very different from anyone who hasn't been there] . . . You've really paid your dues, and you have nothing left to prove, nothing left to lose. They see you like a hero, like a major league ball star, like special. Even the big shots want to come up close to you, maybe to rub against you so it will rub off on them, that something special . . . I have something they *cannot* ever have . . . As bad as my life is now, I wouldn't give up that experience for nothing . . . I have the edge—it's mine, it's me. I just thought of something—I bet that's why boys like me go to war, to have that—that is, being a man. You're better than any major league player, because it was real, no fucking rules, down and dirty, realer than anything anybody else has ever had—if you're alive, that's the gamble, [then] it's yours to keep forever and you can keep it forever. It's yours like nothing else can ever be, and other guys sense it.

Combat veterans mistrust and resent those who try to usurp the test of combat. They are often enraged at noncombatants who claim combat experience in Vietnam. They can spot them easily, "the shiny camo' fatigues, they're surplus store killers" (R.O.). Another Marine: "Those guys in Saigon, drinking cold beer, getting laid and we are out in the bush . . . If I hear them say that they had really been in-country, I would really fuck them up" (E.P.).

Some veterans feel similarly about those who write books about them and Vietnam; they may like the recognition but are fearful that their unique experiences will become too diluted, spread out to include those who write about or read about the war. These veterans were in the war; the war continues inside of them, and many so identified themselves with it, that they *became* the war. They resent anyone who pretends to know the war by hearing or reading *about it,* rather than having *lived it,* having owned the war as they did.

Having lived it is like being anointed, but sharing the feeling of a band of brothers comes at a great price. If they have heard about the "purity of arms" applied to soldiering, they have recognized it as coming from a general or someone who had viewed combat only at a distance. But they maintain that their absolute fidelity to their buddies did have "purity," a belief that is strengthened rather than corroded with time. A war remembered at its best gave ordinary people "the sense of what they were capable of. When they meet some old buddy they . . . talk about the old days . . . [when] they were better men who amounted to more than they do now. It's a precious memory" (Terkel 1984, p. 68).

Anthony Lake, who was President Clinton's national security advisor, is a scholarly man who negotiated peace in Bosnia. He was a U.S. State Department specialist and noncombatant during the Vietnam War, but on one occasion, he carried a weapon as he rode through a combat area. He remembers that he had "the hope that someone would fire at us" so that he could fire back. He doubts that he could shoot another person, but "at that moment I was emotionally prepared to do so." The memory makes him uncomfortable, the *New York Times* reporter notes, but as he reminisced, he recognized that he may not have wanted to kill somebody but was caught up in the arousal of combat: "There is nothing more powerful than a weapon that could take someone's life . . . It was a sort of 'welcome to the human race moment'" (DeParle 1995, p. 35).

AFTER THE WAR

For the poet Yeats, even when "a man is fighting mad," blinded by the realities of war, there may be moments when he "stands at ease, laughs aloud, his heart at peace" (Yeats 1997b). For some men who returned from war, peace indeed does cycle back eventually, but for others war becomes perpetual, such men often battle peace if they have no other enemy. With the end of war, after the celebration of victory, men have found that their peacetime lives are empty.

"Men in their sixties and seventies sit in their dens and recreation rooms around America and know that nothing in their life will equal the day they parachuted into St. Lo" (Broyles 1984, p. 55). A French woman who starved and was fearful all through World War II compares her past and present and sees her life now as "utterly boring." Using the same words as combatants, she said that she does not want war but remembers that "it made me feel alive, as I have not felt alive before or since" (Gray 1970, p. 217).

Returned soldiers realize that all that mattered in combat, friendship and sacrifice, along with combat quickness, strength, aggressiveness, all that is learned to survive in the most hostile world, is not important in peace. After hearing the initial stories of the war, the family wants only to get on with a "normal life." Most families eventually tire of the talk of the war and cannot connect to the experience of combat about which their sons or daughters feel so singularly passionate. And veterans know that some of what happened cannot be told to families without terrible consequences. "They should have left us there . . . or killed us . . . We should have died in Vietnam, the boys, us, me . . . lots of chances to do that. We think about it now. Anyway this [peacetime] life is killing me slowly. But what kind of life could we really have after all that? It had in it all the truth I know" (E.B.).

Former combatants still want the public to acknowledge their unique experience but realize now that they have received nearly all they will get. "Vietnam is used up," one veteran said sadly in 1990 (D.K.). It is painful when the family seems no longer interested in a history that remains the center of the veteran's life. Veterans share their thoughts mostly with each other.

They were young and therefore susceptible to the wonder and unlimited freedom found in war. Some continue to feel that they have been led astray and afterward castigated by their country for their fidelity to each other and to the nation. It has changed them forever. They see a failure on the part of the nation to reaffirm the ancient mutual loyalty between a nation and its warriors at war's end with final honors (Bataille 1986); that, they feel, might have knitted the fracture line.

They were awed by war's constant changes and wonder, but they had absolute clarity, certainly not about war's larger purpose—even our leaders could not articulate that—but in what they had to do for their friends to survive in it. Peace presents ambiguity, complexity, seemingly empty and deceptive rules, codes of conduct, social interactions. Force and brotherhood remain all there is for many of them, and sad numbers of them have died too soon after coming home. With the war long past, they have to keep remembering where they are—now—and the struggle to do that is not always won.

LeRoy G. Schultz
Emeritus Professor
West Virginia University
Morgantown, WV 26506

CHAPTER NINE

SEX AND THE SOLDIER

Fear has a smell
As love does.

—Margaret Atwood, *Surfacing*

Mortal risk heightens sexual arousal; danger survived becomes mortised with the erotic. Such reminiscence is blunted, reshaped, and faded with time but still lurks in memory, remarkably available and trenchant, a tracer reawakening hot feelings.

An eighty-one-year-old woman, a cardiac patient, described a sexual encounter in 1936, during the Spanish Civil War. She subsequently married that man, and they soon divorced. He died some years ago.

> It was in Madrid . . . We knew Franco's troops were coming but we were in the bar in
> a hotel. I thought now we really must get out and escape, but we went to my room and
> made love! Of all things! He was very good.
>
> I could hear small arms fire, then a machine gun going off at a distance. I can remember it all, every bit. Something was burning in the street, I can [still] smell it. He
> was very good. (T.N.P.)

Mortal threat engages all of the senses. Samuel Johnson, impressed with the conversation he had with a friend about to be hanged, famously commented about how "nothing focuses the attention quite like the walk to the gallows." Winston Churchill found that "nothing in life is so exhilarating as to be shot at without effect." With palpable danger, increased sensory arousal often promotes a generally heightened sexuality. The counter is true also. Amid high sexual excitement, physical aggression and pain can become charged with the erotic. Bloodletting and penetration can exert claim on erotic intentions.

In a striking photograph in a restaurant in Sicily, a hunter gazes languidly into the camera, tenderly cradling the head of the deer he has killed. The small animal is surrounded by a bed of pine branches, perhaps to hide the blood, but the overall effect is a view of a shared bower, quiet, restful, and a bit sad. It is a postcoital tristesse.

KILLING AND THE EROTIC

In one respect war is like love, though in no other. Both leave us intervals of rest; and in the intervals life goes on perfectly well without them, though the imagination still dallies with their possibility.

—William James, "Remarks at a Peace Banquet"

Just as the bliss of erotic love

is conditioned by its transiency,

so life is sweet [*in war*] because of the threats of death that envelop it.

—J. Glenn Gray, *The Warriors: Reflections on Men in Battle*

The green combatant lives in constant terror, and even the seasoned soldier is jerked back to that extreme fear by attack, by incoming fire. With contact, the unbearable tension of waiting ends with explosive release. After the furious seconds or minutes of a firefight are over, soldiers revel in the discovery of being alive and with friends. The celebration is for life shared with comrades, rather than for life solely owned. Individuals-become-comrades fuse their lives in battle.

Sexuality is embraced by war. In the grip of mortal danger, there is intoxication and wantonness. Aggression often replaces sexual feeling and bends sexuality into its own aim. Killing itself becomes sexualized:

"Christ, I got off on it, killing . . . collecting ears. . . . I thought, more than once, back then 'I'd rather fight than screw.' Is there something the matter?" (O.I.)

"Sex? There are better things. A kill at a 'klick' [kilometer]. Oh, God, that's better than sex. I can remember it and bring it back. I get off on it, even the memory." (V.E.)

"I had been firing, in an ambush [of Vietcong]. I saw them fall; when I put in a new clip, I saw that I had a hard-on." (R.T.)

One journalist-correspondent made a cassette of the stunning sounds of heavy exchange of fire and used it to seduce women (Herr 1977).

For the combatant in control of the encounter, the moment before squeezing the trigger can be fulsome and erotic. Lust is part of killing in battle, but it is not pretty or romantic. Combat is sexy in the way a weapon is sexy. "Going over the top" was called "sexy" by a British officer in a novel of World War I; not like sex in bed, but far harder, sharper, as in an urgent meeting in a most dangerous liaison (Barker 1996). A man so fearful that he soils himself, may, in the next moment, have an erection. Man becomes a weapon. Gun becomes hard-on. When the gun is a hard-on, the feeling for the target is hardly tender; rather, it is the excitement generated by sexualized dominance. Looking at pictures of dead bodies is like looking at pornography, trying to see more of what is there (Herr 1977), and pornography excites in the use of the sexual object through coercive force, rather than by wooing. Subordinating another by force is said to be exciting, Freud noted, because there is no anxiety coming from the possibility of rejection (Freud 1959).

For some soldiers, this excitement, arousal, and pleasure can later become a source of concern and doubt. In peacetime reflection, it seems abnormal, bizarre. A former Marine combatant confesses: "The first time I killed, I puked and I messed myself, I swear . . . The fifth man I killed . . . I got off on it, I got hard . . . Now if that is normal, what kind of animals are we?" (R.M.). In *The Thin Red Line*, a novel about World War II by James Jones, a group of soldiers finds a bloody shirt, the first sign they have seen of combat death. They touch it, discuss it, look around for more signs of killing and are described as "having a sullen look of sexual guilt. Nobody seemed to want to meet anybody else's eyes. They looked curiously like a gang of boys caught masturbating each other" (Jones 1962, p. 67). Soldiers frequently describe such guilty pleasures.

In combat, delight in destroying can assume an "ecstatic character," an appeal to which we are all susceptible to some degree. For the killer-soldier, "it becomes a consuming lust that swallows up other pleasures. It tends to turn men in on themselves and make them inaccessible to more normal satisfactions" (Gray 1970).

WAR AS SEXUAL ENTERTAINMENT

Me ne frego. [I jack off on (war).]
> —An expression from World War I, adapted by Gabriele d'Annunzio for
> Italian fascism (Woodhouse 1998)

Large audiences consume portrayals of combat and war as entertainment. There is always a market for stories about the male adventurer, and steady readers are familiar with terms such as "penetrate," "insert," and "thrust" into an enemy position and to "withdraw" or "extract" after engagement.

A best-selling book series, *Rogue Warrior*, by Richard Marcinko, tells the story of a commander of "Navy SEAL Team Six" (Marcinko and Wiseman 1993). He describes his counterterrorist task as "hunting" and "killing"; it is presented as adventure and unabashed fun. His group is invariably given an impossibly dangerous mission, so that he must "rewrite the book" on tactics and strategy to survive and succeed. He is the maverick, the rogue, who does everything his way, and he will not obey any other person's rules. Because of his competence and strength, the Navy brass keep out of his way. He recruits his own fiercely loyal, tight buddies who have the same will and strength for the sharp edge of adversity. They respond to any attack on them with satisfyingly effective counterforce. The author-hero has all the strength and potency needed to subordinate any other man who comes up against him. The hero can "fuck him up," dominating him the way he would dominate a woman, a supermasculinity demonstrated in the most difficult contests. Sex is wrapped within his aggression.

Their continuous verbal sparring is sexually tinged, further assurance of the raw male power of Marcinko's band. The reader senses an implication of homophilia but that is also mastered. Their affection for each other comes out of respect for established toughness. Having demonstrated that the competent, powerful warrior can fuck anybody, they do not want to compete in an attempt to dominate each other sexually. They have "safe sex," the safety being in the certainty that they will not cross the boundary with each other, and the sparring always leaves the friend with his manhood intact. It is only the enemies who are fucked and reduced to women. Marcinko writes for men the equivalent of the romance novels designed for women.

HOMOPHILIA

We joke sometimes about how we are queer for each other.

—E.P.

The bonding that develops early in training becomes stronger in combat and is closer for many soldiers than any relationship they can remember before or since. They usually do not express it directly; such revelation is dangerous and could not be tolerated. When soldiers say it, they do so awkwardly and indirectly, often fumbling for the words to describe the inordinate regard and love felt toward one another. One British soldier in the trenches of World War I noted that outsiders would not understand or respect the fullness of his feeling: "They can say what they like; but we are a bloody fine mob" (Winter 1979, p. 186).

When the peacetime commandment against killing is dismissed, the homophobic rule is elevated to the strongest one in war. Yet among the diminishing number of Vietnam veterans, there is enduring closeness, one to the other. Combat has aroused in them a tenderness and concern for trusted comrades, and they are often surprised and awed by such great feelings for other men. Such intense friendship and shared feelings can make them anxious; they joke to defend against any homosexual implication.

This feeling is a stronger version of the bond professional athletes express. While introducing his former center, Mike Webster, to an audience of sportswriters, retired Pittsburgh Steelers quarterback Terry Bradshaw joked: "I loved him from the very first moment I put my hands under his butt" (Seabrook 1997).

Expressing affection to a comrade comes easily when soldiers know that they are about to die together. In the moment before an attack, a British lieutenant and his orderly pause on the fire step of the trench. The orderly kisses him and says in his ear, "Till the very last, Lieutenant" (Winter 1979).

Soldiers sometimes refer to closest and trusted friends as "asshole buddies" (an alternative to "tight buddy"). That is, perhaps, a psychological strategy—to intimidate other men who would be made less certain of their male hardness by such risky and assertive direct reference.

Crossing the line between loving the man who shares hardship and having sex with him sometimes happens, but it is not publicly admitted. The military has strong rules and understood attitudes toward homosexual interaction. It is traditionally judged to be disruptive to group cohesion; the soldier with a personal allegiance to a lover may be less obedient to command and less loyal to the group.

But war makes soldiers extend their limits, and often in combat anything goes. It is also not surprising that it happened in Vietnam: "Marines making love to each other (smile), yeah, you knew who, you looked away" (E.P.). Marines making love may be a rare event but not unknown.

A veteran of the Pacific war reflects on old-timers in the army who had their boyfriends, "None of this buggering was considered homosexual by anyone and authority turned a blind eye to it" (Jones 1962). British officers in World War I privately spoke about the necessity to not stare at soldiers' bodies. Wilfred Owen wrote a sad erotic ode to the boys whom he saw hammered on the anvil of the Front during World War I:

> Let the boy try along this bayonet blade
> How cold the steel is and keen with the hunger of blood;
> Blue with all malice, like the madman's flash;
> And thinly drawn with famishing for flesh.
> Lend him to stroke these blind bullet leads
> Which long to nuzzle in the hearts of lads,
> Or give him cartridges of fine zinc teeth,
> Sharp with the sharpness of grief and death.
> For his teeth seem for laughing round an apple.
> There lurk no claws behind his fingers supple;
> And God will grow no talons at his heels,
> Nor antlers through the thickness of his curls.
>   —Wilfred Owen, "Arms and the Boy"

Homoerotic activity in combat is not always tender; sometimes, although not often, it is rape. The soldier judged to be weakest in the group can be attacked and even sexually violated. He has no place to report the offense. The act degrades him by stamping him absolutely with a boy's worst fear: he is nothing; that is, he is "pussy." It is done to humiliate him and to assert the absolute hypermale power of the perpetrator. It asserts the hardest edge of the soldier's prerogative: if you can fuck someone, do it.

This mix of tenderness and cruelty was also found in Charleston, South Carolina, at the Citadel, where the old values of an all-male military school have been challenged by the court-ordered admission of women. There has been change and an initial angry response in defense of the important values that might be lost. One fear is that the presence of women would ruin the particular relationship and bonding that occurs between men in an all-male environment. As the commandant put it: "We hug each other . . . kisses on the cheek . . . It's like a true marriage. There's an affectionate intimacy between cadets" (Faludi 1994, p. 79).

Along with such intimacy, however, there is a directed cruelty toward lower classmen. Pat Conroy's novel *The Lords of Discipline* came from his experience as student cadet. In it, he says that the experience taught him "the exact kind of man I didn't want to be" (Conroy 1980). Freshmen were addressed as "pussies" and "skirts" until they earned the position of belonging to the fraternity of men. Upper-class "guards" knocked the soap from naked "knobs," first-year cadets, as they were forced to run a gauntlet. As a knob leaned over to pick up the soap, an upperclassman unzipped his pants, saying, "We'll use you the way we used those girls" (Faludi 1994, p. 80). Although this was never officially approved behavior, it was tolerated. Many cadets frequent a transvestite bar in Charleston; many self-described "drag queens" have had sexual liaisons with the cadets. One transvestite performer reported that his cadet told him, "'You're more of a woman than a woman is.'" He goes on to say, "It's like all of us [cross-dressers] are female illusionists and they are male illusionists. A man in uniform is a kind of dream" (Faludi 1994, p. 69).

The dream is the "dreamy" man of a girl's fantasies. It is also a male dream. Boys are to be shaped into the unreal and idealized image of a hard man, unemotional and unflinching. The corresponding ideal image for female behavior is reciprocally soft and compliant to forceful men. The "female illusionist" who is "more woman than a woman" is not playing the role of a real individual woman but rather the role of the ideal, compliant, soft, enticing female as a complementary opposite to the role of hard soldier (Faludi 1994, p. 81).

LOVE OF DOMINANCE

Killing a man who would kill you is a naked self-assertion: "You are dead, I'm alive." Soldiers who exercise such force often become absorbed in this affirmation of potency. It becomes intoxicating and can substitute for sexual union. Sex with tenderness becomes less desired, and the exercise of force becomes most important. There is an addictive aspect to the continued pursuit of this dominating position. It often remains after combat is over.

Writing of his personal experiences in the European war in 1943, J. Glenn Gray says mysteriously, "Sexual passion . . . and the lust for battle are closely akin" (Gray 1970, p. 68). Battlefield lust, that is, excitement in the use of force, and sexual lust spring from the same source. The enemy as partner is to be subordinated repetitively, a new one replacing the downed man: "The sexual partner is not actually destroyed in the encounter, merely overthrown" (Gray 1970, p. 68). Love of dominance easily becomes all of lust.

Sex in the clutch of war is usually hard and aggressive toward women. Rape of civilian women, enemy or not, is more common than admitted (Morris 1996). There is also sometimes love in battle, for example, with women who have been caught in war. But after such human contact, the soldier recognizes the necessity for reaffirming his internal hardness for continuing combat (Boyd 1994).

Tim O'Brien wrote a "peace story" about a grunt who goes AWOL (absent without leave) and finds a Red Cross nurse with whom, over time, he makes love, intensely. He rejoins his unit in combat and he tells of his affair. A buddy asks why he did it, why come back, why so hot to get killed? The soldier says, "All that peace, man, it felt so good it hurt. I want to hurt it back" (O'Brien 1990).

There is no universal male wish to dominate all women, turning them into male-dominated objects of aggression and sexual lust. But war forces the soldiers' exclusive love of itself—war is all force and domination and therefore the soldier makes that the total of loving. In its escalation, the individual combatant's state of mind does not preserve peacetime attitudes about human dignity, compassion, and human relationships. In war, there is only friend and enemy, the dominator and dominated—determined by the strength of desire and firepower.

Men are deeded greater physical strength by evolution and greater political power through our social history. For many individuals and groups, war, active or potential, has served as a continuing reminder that men may have to use that force against other men, possibly to die for their women and kill other men for them. That male idea, related to war, spoken about by some men, is perhaps present but not conscious in others and shapes a social view of the relations between the sexes, even in peacetime.

FUCK

I'm going to turn you into my girlfriend.

—Mike Tyson, to his opponent at weigh-in

Most boys' lives include some victories and some defeats at the hands of other boys. When a boy cries and complains that another boy has hurt him, his parents may comfort him, but often they will instruct him to fight his own battles. Most boys achieve a modicum of confidence in their fighting ability, still envying the mythic champion who never loses. Men watch the skilled athlete, the champion, to share the victory, to identify with his confident manhood and sexual potency. Domination leads to pleasure, satisfaction, "the buzz," "the pump," which are felt by men in both doing and, vicariously, in seeing others dominate in sport and in combat.

Boxing is "the sport to which all others aspire" (Oates and Halpern 1988). Boxing is man against man, each trying to damage the other so that, at the end, the winner dominates the loser. Mike Tyson says that he can change his opponent into a woman permanently because he can really "fuck up" the other man, reduce his will, and hammer him into a woman's perceived passivity. Iron Mike is not making a homosexual advance; his boast is about his possession of physical power, his capacity to dominate and fuck whomever he wishes, his ability to stake out the boundaries of the contest for his opponent. That is hypermale behavior.

Tyson's description of dominance carries far beyond the boxing arena. The image of the destroyed warrior made into a woman and raped is found in ancient Greek literature and in the Hebrew Bible (Niditch 1993). A proto-Nazi drawing of the 1920s illustrates a soldier with a gigantic erection penetrating our planet (Theweleit 1987, 1989). Clausewitz (1984) defined war for nations in the same way: force used to bend the enemy to your will.

Men often say "fuck" as a verbal marker set out for challenge and dominance, and soldiers use the word with great frequency. Soldiers say "fuck" within a sentence and often, as a reflexive stutter, inject it between words or even between syllables: "un-fucking-believable." The soldier may not always attach meaning to the word, as it becomes more and more a verbal habit, a tic. Its constant use, however, starts with the attempt to create distance from civilian, "soft," conventional sentiment. That can be embarrassing: The Marine recruit (E.P.) returned home after boot camp and said at dinner, "Please pass the fucking butter." He asked his surprised family for forgiveness, while simultaneously delineating the newly found difference from his upbringing.

"Fuck you" said to another man, a stranger, is a "throw-down"; it often signals the end of a verbal exchange. It can be a declaration of war, and the man saying it must be ready to fight, not unlike the challenge to "bring 'em on." When women say, "fuck you," it is in imitation, perhaps to shake loose from subordination, to not be cowed, and to manifest self in aggressive mastery and competence at the moment. A woman who says "fuck you" to a strange man presents an unusual and confusing challenge because it is a male challenge and in such situations, with some men, a woman's expected protection against physical attack can evaporate.

Most men want to hold on to love and carry women into battle in memory, as word and as image. In Vietnam, as in other wars, the "grunts," that is, infantry soldiers, "humped" many things. Tim O'Brien, a Vietnam combat veteran, wrote of what men carry in battle: "They were called legs or grunts. To carry something is to hump it." Soldiers hump guns, ammo, and their lives; they also hump photographs of sweethearts. They "hump their love" (O'Brien 1990). They carry the twin burdens of love and terror. "Hump" has the other meaning, but the love of a man in combat is not pure. One recreational songbook of a U.S. Army Air Corps squadron stationed in England during World War II reportedly contained pornoerotic songs with "unprintable lyrics" centering on the synecdochical use of "cunt," with every woman described as a "whore" and including songs about intercourse with a dead woman (French 1992). The airmen shouted these songs at the top of the lungs as marching cadences and in beer halls near military stations as they pounded their fists. The same happened during the Korean War and undoubtedly in all wars.

The grunt going to Vietnam aimed to "fuck up" the enemy and discovered immediately after he arrived that he was fucked by just being in-country. Some soldiers who lost the tether of discipline wanted to "fuck Vietnam" (O'Brien 1994).

In combat, in a state of high arousal with restraints released, merging sexual desire and aggression is complete. The soldier who moves reflexively and forcefully to dominate has the greatest chance of survival. As one veteran said, "Don't you civilians get it? Well, you can't. The world in-country is the fucker or the fucked. I am alive only because I fucked them" (V.E.).

After a firefight: "We really fucked them up." To fuck up the enemy is to kill or maim enough individuals that the unit attacked is deprived of power, subordinated to your own. Exultant after the orgiastic release of a successful firefight, a frenzied soldier shouted: "We fucked them like pussy" (O.I.).

PORNOGRAPHY

> In sadism, long since known to us as a component instinct of sexuality . . . we have before us a particularly strong alloy . . . between trends of love and the destructive instinct . . . In sadism . . . the death instinct twists the erotic aim . . . [to its own purpose] and yet fully gratifies the erotic aim.
>
> —Sigmund Freud, *Three Essays on Sexuality*

Military training is preparation for use of force, and pornography constructs the corresponding sexual frame for the young soldier. In the long history of war, the pornoerotic has continued to color attitudes toward women. Although officially not sanctioned, such attitudes are expected and unofficially encouraged (Morris 1996). The pornoerotic arouses, "gets men up"; that is, it makes them feel their ability at dominating and focuses them on aggression. American aviators were reportedly shown pornographic movies before they flew combat missions in the Gulf War (Kurtz 1991). That is also reportedly a general practice on aircraft carriers even in peacetime, when mortal risk is less extreme but still exists in the dangerous task of launching and landing on a carrier deck with pitch, yaw, and roll. The few women aviators on board the carriers objected, but the practice still continued. Anything that might contribute to the ability of men to do the dangerous tasks well was tolerated.

A notorious example of this behavior occurred at the 1991 Tailhook Convention attended by aircraft carrier personnel in California. The convention invitations showed the logo of the carrier plane and the boast: "We stay up longer and deliver big loads," a not-so-subtle reference to sexual potency. The men wore T-shirts that declared "Women Are Property." Complaints of sexual aggressiveness at the convention finally led to reprimands and forced retirements of personnel up to the admiral level. The impetus to the Tailhook Convention, the spirit of which was supposedly based on the movie *Top Gun*, was its emphasis on the pleasure of the male group in dominance.

When the nation's existence depends on military force, military command may dictate use of any means for the support and expression of male dominance and possible objections from women become unimportant, even if they too are in the military. In peacetime, military commanders are more subservient to the political arm of our nation and must accept their embarrassment over Tailhook incidents. But perhaps they assume, as I have been told, that when the "balloon goes up" and real war starts, things will go back to "normal." Then they will again take charge of shaping the way the population thinks and acts, without regard to irrelevant sensitivities. What is present, then, is not love of intimacy and pleasure but of aggression.

PERVERSION

The sexuality of most male human beings contains an element of aggressiveness— a desire to subjugate; the biological significance of it seems to lie in the need for overcoming the resistance of the sexual object by means other than the process of wooing.

—Sigmund Freud, *Three Essays on Sexuality*

To fuck is not to love. It is colored by sexual meaning while keeping its hard-edged penetrating meaning of domination. This "linking of the erotic with the subjugation of another person can be considered the basic defining boundary of perversion" (Stoller 1986). Perversion resides in the substitution of "using" for "loving." To fuck is to make dead, an assertion of having no other feeling toward the other but dominance. It is also a statement of the deadness that takes over the person who wants only to dominate and cannot, then, love. Absolute power over other human lives is intoxicating. Men in war are at particular risk because they feel intense power, accentuated by the periods of mortal terror that heighten the wish for release, for getting back, for achieving dominance. Some men learn to love it, and those who have discovered that kind of love are surprised and, with time for reflection, shocked at their susceptibility. Perversion can replace usual appetite and leave little room for its recovery.

At the time of enthrallment, there is no concern for the subordinated person who is used to achieve maximal pleasure. In combat, no one and nothing has any value outside of the dominance defined by the power held and the support of loyal friends. Guilt may return in the form of unwanted memories and regret for the former soldier and also for the nation that shares some of the responsibility. Reduction of a human to a "thing" is the essential nature of the pornoerotic; the merging of eroticism with aggression, as described by Freud, was scandalously exemplified in the abuse of male prisoners by male and female guards in Baghdad's Abu Ghraib prison.

LOVE

The only love . . .
—Text on a bumper sticker seen in Boston, overprinted on a map of Vietnam

Combat offered to many men an arresting engagement before they had one with a woman. Some men may not have loved their country because it was too large to be known, and our cause in Southeast Asia was murky and then was lost, but the soldier could love what he discovered the war contained for him. He loved his comrades, he loved the excitement, he may have loved the fact that its dangers could be survived. The bumper sticker presents a profound commentary on war: if Vietnam remains the only love, it endures because it was a place of great emotional attachments, fixed by competing pulls of love, lust, force, terror, and rage, and therefore it eclipses all others.

Some former combatants say that combat ruined them for subsequent relationships with women. Many Vietnam combat veterans have great and continuing difficulty expressing tenderness to their partners. Sex is abrupt, rushed, if it occurs at all. Women are not trusted. Women who become close to them can receive residual aggression from combat: "I can't have comfort now with a woman, and I know I'll never have it again. What I have now is the same rage, the high of anger I had in Vietnam, and it's going to kill me" (N.P., returned veteran, now deceased).

Those at home who protested the Vietnam War endorsed "make love, not war," and the answer written on combatants' jackets was "make war, not love." Rather than a statement of contradiction, it was a mirroring congruence for many soldiers; war had become for them, at that time, love.

It is one of the great paradoxes of war that there is so much love in it. Soldiers love intensely. They love each other, they love their family, and their women. But war in its daily activities is itself pitted against love of all the others outside of war. War powerfully competes with any other love and demands exclusive love of itself. Human love in the sweetness of peace can be one of the many casualties in the lives of former combatants.

PART IV
THE FUTURE OF WAR

WOMEN AND WAR

It is not in giving life but risking life that man is raised above the animal . . . Superiority has been accorded by humanity not to the sex which brings forth life but to that which kills.

—Simone de Beauvoir, *The Second Sex*

Until recently, women have been peripheral to the action of wars, more often serving as auxiliaries and in noncombatant jobs. More recent wars have brought women much closer to the action. Their active role in a nation at war has been only reluctantly recognized; they have been onlookers and cheerleaders. Their exemption from mortal contest has a major social consequence, in war and in peace.

Embedded in the idea of war and in the reality of war is a difference between the sexes. Men and women are brought together as paired opposites—men are warriors, active heroes who risk their lives to protect more passive women. In the history of war, men have protected women from enemy men. Are women essential to the male idea of war and its intrinsic heroism? The mourning of women, it is said, may be necessary for dead heroes (Ezrahi 1997).

We cannot answer the question of nature versus nurture. But, we can observe and seek historical views. We have seen that men feel murder closer to the heart, or they can be pushed to impose real damage more easily than women. They will kill for revenge or to achieve status and respect. That is as true among boys as it is among men in our society and among career criminals, such as mafiosi on the rise who achieve honor through killing. Prestate peoples today still engage in constant warfare for status; their group raids are primarily for "hijacking women." It is a leap to believe that a raw evolutionary force dictates male aggression in the Jivaro and Yanomamo and, as well, in technological societies, but it would also be arrogant not to think of the possibility.

In the male fantasy of war, women offer absolution for the killing at war's end because the combat was for them and, thus, for civilization. This chapter will focus on the differences between men and women seen in war and on conjectures as to the origins of these differences, women's acceptance of men's aggression influenced by the history of war, and the way in which women have always been carried into war as weapon, mother, ideal, prize, and victim.

Women in Western nations have traditionally been raised to be more passive, needing men to protect them. Men have been raised just the opposite. The broadest concept in Western women's political movements is to assert the place of women as able, not helpless, and to emphasize that such helplessness is not nature's directive but a social construction, unnecessary and damaging to women and, ultimately, to society. Feminism shapes the cultural process leading toward parity, rather than allowing physical strength and longstanding social roles to dictate women's social position.

CAN WOMEN WAR?

Scarcely a human in the course of history has fallen to a woman's rifle.

—Virginia Woolf, *Three Guineas*

Women traditionally have sought preservation of life rather than the promised rewards for risking life in mortal conflict. More men want war than do women; war is marked out as a historically and psychologically male place. Women have established less of their own place in the grand history of Western society because they are not the active element in war and those who record history record war. Oliver Wendell Holmes drew the connection between war and history when he stated that every society rests on men's mortal sacrifice (Holmes 1914/2000).

War, and the prospect of war while in peacetime, is at least partly responsible for the subordinate position of women in society in all periods. The respect for women's work during times of war has been quickly retracted in peace. After

World War II, female war production workers were asked to leave their factory and farm jobs and return to domestic activities. Not all did it gladly, but it was expected that they would turn the jobs back to the soldiers who had fought as a patriotic duty. Even women who have taken enemy fire in combat are not always acknowledged. Many women who served as nurses in Vietnam carry continued anger and a sense of betrayal because of public disinterest in their work under fire. After one nurse died in a mortar attack, a group was told, in clear violation of the truth, that they could not have a memorial service for her because "women do not die in Vietnam" (Palmer 1993, p. 41).

Almost all women and many men hope that war will end, but men are acculturated to the belief that part of their dominant social position has, at its base, the possibility of dying in war in defense of women. If war really becomes an equal-opportunity employer and women can become active combatants, that could be pivotal to the general perception of women's place in society.

The lesser upper-body strength of women is a deterrent to women's combat role despite the technology that has made muscle mass a decreasing factor in many aspects of warfare. The best competitive women athletes would function better than average males, but the military cannot depend on recruiting a large number of female Olympic contenders. As war changes, women have taken new responsibilities, but they have not had significant combat roles, even in Iraq. Modern changes in technology and tactics of war level the battlefield, indiscriminately increasing both the vulnerability and the effectiveness of troops, regardless of gender.

Soldiers who cannot keep up, regardless of gender, endanger the lives of others. A unit's ability to survive depends on a full complement of soldiers in many roles. Soldiers are trained to keep the unit together, to leave no soldier behind, and that going back to pick up stragglers can be suicidal. The contradiction is felt deeply by the military, who see disaster to *esprit* in combat units where women are expected to be laggards because of their physical differences.

High levels of military command, the group that passes down orders, also must take orders from political leaders. Resistance to change is a career stopper for those who want to advance and make their place in the higher echelons. They espouse equality, write regulations for equal treatment, create mandatory courses against sexual harassment, but, as might be expected, they secretly share the view that women cannot measure up (Gutmann 1997), even if the women outrank or outcommand them. The difficulty of having women in combat is expressed in terms of logistical proximity, for example, bedding down women in the close space of the carrier or in the still-tighter space of a submarine, the expense and difficulty of separate latrines, not to mention the difficulty in the field when any man's greater speed at urinating is indisputable. (A woman combatant is slower, a "sitting duck.") Those are significant problems, difficult to solve in an integrated service, and may have enormous costs.

The general, infrequently discussed prohibition against women in combat is the conviction of professional soldiers that the job of training for war and waging it must be left to them and the men they lead. War, historically, has been the use of force by men against other men, powered by male aggression. War, military cadre know, is not the equivalent of mixed doubles: international rules of engagement will not require that enemy forces have a similar gender mix. Men are proven combatants; women's capacity to inflict mortal damage on the enemy has not been tested. Women have not been primed to kill, from early childhood, through competition and attachment to weapons (Wood 1991).

Men are expected to die rather than to lose their place as men in the eyes of other men, and often women share that view of manhood. Women have been acculturated to a different position. They can be resolved and aggressive to protect their children, but if overwhelmed, they can concede to save themselves and their child. They have not grown up with "the test."

Command officers are reluctantly involved in the democratic social experiment to acculturate women for war. Even though they may welcome women in noncombatant roles as administrators and officers, many are negative about women in combat roles. Officers understand how men grow up, how to motivate them for combat; they believe that women's entry into combat can compromise future wartime victory. Women must think and act as though all-out war against a determined enemy is always possible. Those who seek social equality for women see the deeper issue as the denial of women's right to risk their lives in combat to serve their country.

Many men and some women would object to removing the differentiated relationship between the sexes established in war. Debate about women combatants has appropriate political moment; it is part of a battle for social change. It reminds us all of our allegiance to equality as a democratic principle. Serious war, that for which the military must always be prepared, has required warriors—men who would rather die than disgrace themselves—who would die to exact vengeance on an enemy. Women generally make less than ideal warriors because they have been acculturated to question what is gained and what is lost by dangerous action and murderous impulse. Women can be oppressed and still retain some self-respect as victims. Men are less able to allow themselves subordination and victim status; they are more likely than women to die before accepting that position.

In the current fight against terrorism, the use of women as soldiers may optimize our chance for success. Women can function in a military future in which there is less need for warriors and more need for those who can manage the increasing complexity of information and skills. The presence of women in many phases of combat is endorsed (Peters 2002). Many Islamic countries have also seen the potential for women in the military.

WOMEN AND WEAPONS

The sexualized relationship between the soldier and his weapon is plainly recognized but not fully understood. The infantryman handles his weapon as a loved object; he cleans and polishes it in training and sleeps with it in combat. Weapons are metaphors, carrying contradictory sexual meanings about women. Women are to be protected; yet, they possess dangerous powers. The soldier's practical need to service his weapon and to make it serve him well is combined with his need for strong magic against combat's constant fear of death. Men carry women into war as fantasized powerful partners. Fantasies of women can make the soldier hard in his attack on the enemy soldier's life and potency.

The Hebrew words for weapons, *klei zayin,* also serve as a slang expression for the male genitals (Ezrahi 1997). Weapons also merge male and female. In the eighteenth and nineteenth centuries, weapons bore ornate, explicitly pornographic decorations (Czerny's International Auction House 2004). *Blunderbuss,* a commonly used German term for musket, was translated as "Brown Betsy" in England, where personal weapons became more elaborate and fitted with highly polished brown stocks. The American frontiersman in turn referred to his rifle as "Betsy." The B-17 that dropped the first nuclear bomb on Hiroshima was named "Enola Gay," after the pilot's mother. The enormous German field gun in use in World War I was called "Big Bertha," after Bertha Krupp, the grande dame of the munitions manufacturing family.

"Betsy" had a new incarnation in the twentieth century. The German antiper-sonnel land mine used in World War II terrified Allied troops because when tripped, it fired a canister containing steel pellets straight up into the air, set to explode at the level of a man's groin. It was called "Bouncing Betsy," perhaps to counter anxiety, perhaps as a reflection of the soldier's conflicted feelings toward women—raw desire for women and fear that contact with women would take their manhood. In Vietnam, VC trip-wire, antipersonnel mines were called "Walking Betsy's" (R.M.) without direct historical reference to the German mines of twenty years before.

The *Oxford English Dictionary* (*OED*) presents a detailed explanation and ar-gument about the derivation of the word *gun* as an example of the common prac-tice of bestowing "hypocoristic," or "pet names," on all the tools of war. The *OED* argues that *gun* was derived from a woman's name: "the pet-name for Gunnhildr in Old Norse would be '*Gunna*,' becoming '*gunne*' in Middle English."[1] Giving women's names for weapons presents an arresting contradiction, suggesting hid-den meaning. It tears the usual assumption in Western culture that women weave the fabric of peace and men make the hard weaponry of war. But the naming cre-ates a powerful emotional synergy: it borrows women's awesome life-giving power and welds it to the killing potential of the weapon bearer. The man hold-ing the weapon has equal or greater power over other men: he can kill or, by re-straint, he can "give life," as a veteran puts it (D.K.).

But men regard the power of women ambivalently (French 1992). In war, women are simultaneously prized, revered, and denigrated. In men's minds, women are a species apart, lusted after and, because of combat's urgent neces-sity, diminished in importance.

WAR IS FOR WOMEN

[*A man's dream is to love*] a good woman and kill a bad man.

—Robert Heinlein, quoted in Grossman, *On Killing*

Women have always been a part of the plunder of warfare. The war at the be-ginning of Western history, narrated in the *Iliad*, was ostensibly fought for Helen. Even in modern nations, men have gone to war feeling that they are risking their lives to protect their women, and thereby their nation and civilization. The soldier holds women in memory tenderly and strongly, as he does his weapon. And there is mistrust of weapons: they may fail him, and the soldier knows that the enemy's weapon is also deadly and perhaps also bears a woman's name.

Before the modern Western state, the spoils of war routinely included women. Women's place in ancient hierarchies was to serve the powerful men as wives and to serve the group as producers of children. The *ban* in the Hebrew Bible, the edict from God to destroy all of the enemy, was relaxed toward virginal women of the enemy, preserving them to produce children who would join in work and war. The ban also reflected the patriarchal value that purity of lineage resided in male seed, while virgin women were viewed as being as alterable as clothing. Women would learn to adjust to a different life among the Israelites. The heads of captured virgin women were shaved and their nails pared; they were given a month to mourn the loss of father and mother before they were reborn and joined the Israelites (Deuteronomy 21:11–14). For the victorious warrior, the process was simple: "to every man a damsel or two" (Judges 5:30).

Peoples such as the Yanamamo (Chagnon 1983), the Jivaro (Harner 1984), and the Dani (Matthiessen 1962) made raids against other tribes for respect among their peers and scarce resources (food, for example). But they most frequently made war for much-needed women. When anthropologist Napoleon Chagnon asked an older Yanomamo warrior, "Why do you fight?" he responded, "Don't ask me such stupid questions! Women! Women! Women! That's what started it! We fought for women."[2]

In perhaps the most famous war in history, Trojans fought against the Achaians with Helen as the prize. Here is Thersites, railing at Agamemnon for his greed:

> What are you panting after now?
> Your shelters packed
> with the lion's share of bronze, plenty of women too
> crowding your lodges. Best of the lot, the beauties
> we hand you first whenever we take some stronghold.
> —Homer 1990, 2:260–70

In war and in peace, states have been "firmly linked to male power," and men at war become a species apart from women. In sustained war, men become the war and the war moves forward through men's actions (Theweliet 1987). Any part given to women is a concession, a tokenism found mostly in recent times. In general, when nations have faced destruction, some women took up arms. The more recent acceptance of women as integral to the military represents a change in views of women and womanhood.

In any event, women's direct participation in war is reluctantly noticed and treated as ancillary to the thrust against the enemy. Women may be allowed to take part, but because men are primed from youth for combat, it is they who are still seen as essential in war.

BEGINNINGS

Sex, it is now thought, began as the simple act of hijacking,

when some billion years ago, a small cell waylaid

and merged with a bigger one, richer in substance and nutrients.

—Sara B. Hrdy, *The Woman That Never Evolved*

This is a guess that, by its nature, is beyond direct proof. But it is an appropriate metaphor for the place of power in male and female relationships. It speaks of the earliest beginning of predation and subordination, of the varied and subtle competitions that permeate the mundane human interactions between men and women.[3]

The strongest, most powerful men in social hierarchies, the despots, have always had the most women. There are severe penalties for the ordinary man who tries to increase his reproductive chances against a leader or despot. In many parts of the world, there were harems of thousands, controlled absolutely by despots. Moulay Ismail is credited with 888 offspring from his four wives and great numbers of concubines. In Dahomey, the despots who ruled the country had access to all the women; other men were not permitted to have sexual relations with those women (Betzig 1986). We can assume that other Dahomey men did find a way, despite the threat of punishment.

Women have been physically and politically overwhelmed into accepting male domination, but they resist when resistance is possible. In all animals, including humans, male tyranny over females decreases with monogamy (Betzig 1986), and monogamy is the usual standard in democracies. In present-day Western states, men's past control over women's reproduction has become increasingly more a battle of equals—for example, in the right to choose to continue a pregnancy.

WAR IS AGAINST WOMEN

A world of clerks and teachers, of coeducation . . . and "associated charities," of feminism unabashed. No scorn, no hardness, no valor anymore! Fie upon such a cattleyard of a planet.

—William James, *The Moral Equivalent of War*

War is against an enemy, but it is also a battle of men against values usually assumed to be female and, ultimately, against the woman within.

In war, the cannon has had voice, men have had voice, the silent sword has had voice, but women rarely have had voice. Clausewitz's spare definition—"war is merely the continuation of policy with other means" (Clauswitz 1984, p. 87)—elegantly frames war with purpose and omits its horror, but Clausewitz also reminds us that the "other means" is force: "War is thus an act of force to compel our enemy to do our will" (p. 75). After all the talking, negotiating, and rational calculating are done, those who make war want to impose a basic, simple dichotomy of dominator and subdued. That holds the center of much, not all, of what really matters between humans. War has subjugation at its center, and that idea of war has shaped the intertwined lives of women and men in peace.

Women were pronounced "sexually unfit to fight a war" by one English journalist in 1915 (Hynes 1991). That view underlies current policies, as reflected in reports from a country like Israel where women are drafted for service, but, contrary to common belief, are generally restricted from combat service (Bagatell et al. 1994). The potential for war, and the responsibility for men as soldiers to execute the will of the nation by going to war, is part of the background for female subordination. In peace, word and image refresh memories of the heroism of men who kill other men and die to protect the nation's women. Marinetti, a founder of Italian "futurism" and fascism, declared in 1909: "We wish to glorify War; the only health-giver in the world—militarism, patriotism, the destructive arm of the Anarchist, the beautiful Ideas that kill, the contempt for women" (Hynes 1991, p. 7). Such ideas became the beginning of Italian fascism in 1919 (Payne 1995). Whatever their virtues appreciated at other times, the role given to women when war starts or is about to start has been to encourage the fight. During World War I, pretty women volunteers in England were assigned to give white feathers (a symbol of cowardice) to any young man they saw not in uniform, as if to say, "Are you so feeble as not to kill strangers in my defense?" (Gullace 1997).

De Beauvoir's epigram about the relative worth of men and women builds on a still-larger historical truth; social acclaim is most often given to the risktaker, the dominator, and the life taker. Those who do the necessary work for continuity in society, whether men or women, remain in the background. A military historian, Ralph Peters, writing about battle with Islamists, lists their demeaning of women as one of the attributes that will make their cause a failure (Peters 1997).

A U.S. soldier badly wounded in World War II described how his rejection of the feminine disappeared after German ordnance took away half a buttock and put a metal shard in his head. In an echo of the thesis presented earlier regarding the psychological roots of fascism, he described how his father gave him a legacy of guns and the denial "of the juices in yourself . . . [the necessity] to treat women as a piece of ass." Father's injunction was "to be hard . . . otherwise you will be destroyed on the killing grounds of life." All his life, until he was wounded, was devoted to "get the woman" out of his system. Her "juices" could leach away his manhood, wash him into neutered nothingness (Wood 1991, p. 65). His wound, he says, finally gave him, at great cost, the right of manhood with the voice to acknowledge a shared humanity with women (Wood 1991, p. 65). Exclusive male bastions, such as the military and some boys' schools, strongly shape boys to choose to be the dominator or the dominated. A memoir about a boy's school in which beatings by other boys made the writer a deliverer of beatings as well, forced on him the realization that an exclusively male authority is "the solvent of humanity." Beatings shaped a school into the landscape of combat, a society of the subordinated and the dominated (Jerome 1994).

In war, victory comes from superior force skillfully wielded: the results of the Tailhook Convention reinform us that men's attachment to war comes at least partly out of the love for the exercise of such power as a male prerogative. The potential for exerting group force in peace resides in male environments or when groups of men are alone. It is expressed in language and jokes that give respect to force alone, lessening and extinguishing regard for those without it. A T-shirt worn at the Tailhook Convention in 1991 stated on its front "Women Are Prop-

erty," and on the back, "He-man Woman Hater's Club." Borrowed from a popular TV show, *Married, with Children,* this slogan expressed a prevalent military
attitude despite the official condemnation of the demeaning of women in the
military services. Military command in this nation is given the difficult task of
following regulations derived from democratic attitudes, including respect for
the weak, which are inimical to military purpose and customs. Democracy and
respect, for example, are in opposition to training that demands compliance and
celebrates dominating strength and contempt for weakness. Clausewitz (1984)
defined war variously but referred to force at its center; yet, he also warned
against command abrogating the political rules and ethos of the nation it serves
and becoming a law unto itself. But military command in our nation, aware of
such contradictions, also must fear that the battle for social change may reduce
the capability to respond to attack with dominating force.

WOMEN'S POWER

Disorder does not come from Heaven, but rather from women.

—Confucius

Men at war savagely want women. Deprivation raises desire, and the constant
fear of the soldier's own death fuels it. A woman can allay both deprivation and
fear. Women's power resides in their sexual desirability and in their ability to
withhold or to give themselves. They hold the magic of life and the total body
comfort given by mother (Balint 1939). The Hebrew Bible presents, in the midst
of bloody narratives of war, occasional suggestions of ways to reconcile with enemies, including offering former enemies "women spoil" (Judges 21:13, as quoted
in Niditch 1993). Sex is healing and unifying (DeWaal 1989).[4] Because women
have such power to heal and soothe, they are a danger *to* war; they can corrupt
men's partnership in it. Soldiers are cautioned about women; women are popularly mythified as the deceptive and powerful tricksters who rob a soldier of
strength in battle.

Soldiers are shaped by training to look on women with lust because other feelings would soften resolve, distract, seduce into longing, and compete dangerously with vigilance and attention to comrades. Men at war tell of the fight
against fantasies, reveries about women. In such fantasies, there are rapid shifts

of persona. Women also become the enemy, their allure competing with soldiers' bonding to comrades. Tender thoughts of women can seduce men into sleep and death.

The frustration of the young soldier's sexual need easily smolders into rage. Amid aggressiveness toward the enemy, the excruciating boredom and fear in waiting for contact, some of that rage is toward the absent woman not there to comfort.

Men engage in contests for women as prizes. Men who have lost the love of a woman to another man may be angry with him, indeed even murderously so, but moral condemnation is usually reserved for the woman he lost. Wartime comradeship, without this direct contest for a woman, is made strong partly for that reason. Death faced in the exclusive company of comrades, solely directed toward killing enemy men, leads to a shared enduring conviction that absolute safety is found only with comrades. No woman, after one's mother, can provide its equal.

The story of Samson and his betrayal by Delilah, of another tribe, is the best-known cautionary biblical tale about women (Judges 13–16). Warriors are warned that women are dangerous and that it is their nature to use their attractions to deceive. They may be of the enemy or could join the enemy side—their loyalty is never that of comrades (Ehrenreich 1989).

Delilah tricks Samson into revealing his secret, and then she takes his great strength by cutting his hair. He is put in chains, blinded, now "eyeless in Gaza," and mocked because a woman has taken his power. Samson saves himself as a man only by exercising the final option: he uses his secretly regained strength to destroy all of his enemies and himself. By sacrificing his life, he recaptures his manhood and God's approval.

Judges also contains the story of the woman Jael, who lures the exhausted enemy warrior, Sisera, into her tent, gives him the comfort of warmth and milk, then kills him with a woman's domestic tool: she hammers a tent peg into his temple (Judges 4, 18).

THE WAR AGAINST WOMAN: FASCISM

The concern about the female body subverting the masculine imperative was a dominant theme of Nazi militarism. Love of women constituted a danger to the German man—to the soldier and the "myth of the male body."

Tannhauser, a Teutonic knight, has occupied a central position in Germanic myth. Tannhauser desired the goddess Venus and finds his wish answered—he lived inside her mountain retreat, surrounded by comforts. In her dark, wet world, Venus and her naiads constantly attend his sexual desire. Wagner's opera begins with Tannhauser's lament, a declaration of his great struggle against lubricious pleasures. The hero finally wins his battle against the lulling softness of women with an act of will—he resolves to leave the soft paradise and be reborn as a man in the world of men and war. To do that, he declares himself ready for battle, "even for death and nothingness." He embraces the brilliant hard lightning of war, renouncing the dark fluid environment of the goddesses' world under the mountain, the murky grottoes, dim pools, and misty waterfalls (Gilmore 1990). He has taken himself away from the soothing of women's bodies. He craves only metal next to his skin and the company of his warrior comrades. He successfully throws off his past desire for the quiet soothing underground bower and sets about his return to the hard clash of war. The Nazi movement's beginnings was in the *Freikorps,* a group of loosely organized German freebooters who refused to surrender after World War I. They left behind their recorded history and hundreds of novels that illuminate their thinking (Theweleit 1987).

They continued to fight Bolshevism through the 1920s and embraced war as necessary and continuous for the male assertion of dominance over the feared feminine. Theweleit argues that the Nazis were threatened from the inside by their bodies' softness and from the outside by women's seductiveness. Men wage a chronic struggle to separate their bodies from women's absolutely. Theweleit conjectured that the individual struggle was the major part of the Nazis' continuing push toward war. The fascist culture was directed toward the attempt to shape a man into an image with skin as hard as metal armor. For fascists, an ideal man was a persevering, uncompromising, dutiful, and unfeeling soldier. National Socialism offered little else of any additional political ideology. The fantasy of the hard male body was elevated to a primary position that defined the Nazi ethos. The major political polarization of gender can be seen as the start of the adventure of fascism: war against the world to demonstrate the hardness of the German soldier's body in contrast to the female of other nations. The ideal German soldier "[who] could not be debrutalized," as Goering stated, would bend others to his will—the same as the will of the leader and Germany.

In that psychological and socially enforced construction, a "pure race" is a *male* race; women are separated from such ambitions because they are associated with softness and dirt. They function in the Nazi world as producers of male soldiers and workers. Although Theweleit's (1987, 1989) analysis started exclusively with the historical literature of the Nazi movement and clearly points to German cultural traits, such as absolute obedience to authority and racial superiority, there remains the troubling perception that the German form of fascism elaborated and made a historical reality of male fantasies about women can still be found.

Many men are attracted to this centering idea of the Nazi movement—the rejection of the feminine within themselves—as seen in the prevalence of skinheads here and abroad. The completed fantasy is to transmogrify the body of the fascist male into the hardness of metal armor; or an organized phallic body—man becomes weapon—as if without internal organs, the man of the superrace finds his apotheosis as part of the war machine. Women are lesser and dirty, necessary as machines who serve only to produce little soldiers (Theweleit 1987).

Loving that "which makes you hard" states the nature of affection allowed within Nazi mythology: in a continuing state of war, comrades are the fixed point in consciousness, and the contract with them cannot be broken. The affection for comrades must be stronger than that for a woman. In the world of constant war, closeness to a woman is transient; even in the midst of sexual intimacy, the ear must be attuned to the bugle's call. A woman, other than mother, is loved only because she makes the man hard enough for penetration.

The soldier's fight is against his longing for mother's omnipotence and warmth, which threatens the soldier's strength and existence. An indoctrinated German soldier wrote that during his cadet training, "I found any kind of solicitous care quite intolerable, and the broad stream of my mother's empathy made me wish to breathe the harsher air of the Corps again" (Theweleit 1989, p. 151). The soldier's battle is against his desire for proximity with women, and the woman most proximal is inside him. It is waged in comradeship with other men.

THE PORNOEROTIC VIEW OF WOMEN IN WAR

The soldier's ambivalence toward women sharply distinguishes the woman as prostitute who must submit to his force from the distant, pure woman at home—mother or virgin bride. The prostitute is despised, reviled, and treated as an enemy; the sexual act is aggressive penetration: she is fucked.

William Manchester described killing an enemy soldier in World War II. Afterward, an enemy shell kills members of his platoon. He finds a hole and, exhausted, sleeps. He has a dream that has, despite its hallucinatory content, a strong feel of reality. In the dream, a woman appears, a trickster, a *jinn*, changing shape and identity in increasingly exciting forms. She finally becomes the provocative "whore of death," a frightening image, but when she winks at him, he becomes hard. When she speaks, "the key words were blood and lust and death." She opens her legs and says that they will have sex at the Japanese lines. He resists, knowing he would die in her embrace, touches himself, and comes almost immediately (Manchester 1979, p. 73).

He had killed and felt guilty about the excitement and the juxtaposition of that thrill of killing with the death of his comrades. He is profoundly tired, shaken, and his dream at once condenses all of his anxiety and erases its tension with sexual climax.

RAPE

War is said to be fought for women back home, but it also preserves the social power of men over women. The making of war always involves tension between the release of repressed aggression and the need to contain soldiers within a rule of law. Susan Brownmiller presented the idea that male aggression and its manifestation in rape is a conscious process of intimidation by which *all men* keep *all women* in a state of fear (Brownmiller 1975). The level of interest in rape—real or potential—as the personal desire of a man or men is debatable, but it is clear that few men rape even when they can, that training for war overrides individual social restraints, and that more men rape when war poses the probability of their own death (Morris 1996).

The rape of women in Bosnia was intended to make them pariahs. Such acts were an amalgam of simple lust powerfully combined with declared national purpose to demean and to destroy the emotional center of the enemy. Leaders created a climate that justified the abuse of physical power over women.

A veteran of the Gulf War told me about raping a U.S. woman soldier as the order to advance against the enemy was finally given (R.D.). The intense anxiety felt by the man initiated the need to reverse the terror of meeting a possibly over-powering force by subordinating another, thus proving that "I am not weak, you are. I can fuck you." This soldier had been sexually assaulted and shamed as a boy and spoke about the need for forceful assertion of sexual identity. The attack on the woman was that soldier's recourse for assertion of personal strength in the midst of the terror of vulnerability. It was a declaration of dominance and mastery and a rejection of personal softness, of his passive position waiting for attack himself. In World War II, military rape in the combat theaters rose far above civilian levels. With increased forward troop movement in the "breakout" preceding the end of German resistance (March and April 1945), there was more extensive contact with civilians; incidents of crime or aggravated assault and rape by U.S. troops increased dramatically. Rape in combat areas was often punished lightly because it was seen as less serious than murder.[5]

Rape may be the most underreported violent crime, even in peacetime. This is another indication of attitudes toward relationships between men and women, according privilege to male strength and the understanding that "boys will be boys," particularly "sexually deprived" boys who are soldiers. As a result, rape in war was treated by the command as an understandable response of fighting men often without "real harm done," compared with the soldier's daily expo-sure to violent death. But restrictions on brutality are in uneasy proximity to the exhortation to soldiers to fight, imposing on command the dual task of con-demning brutality while pushing for victory.

The wartime rates of rape by soldiers decrease in peacetime to or below civil-ian levels. Entering the military in peacetime imposes a highly structured, regu-lated life, with monitoring of activities and enforcement of regulations. But the military group ethic also fosters solidarity through violence and the idealization of the "hypermasculine" (Shatan 1977).[6] The risk of soldiers engaging in indi-vidual or group rape becomes significant, especially if external deterrents are minimized by those in charge.[7]

POWER AND WOMEN

Power is the greatest aphrodisiac.

—Henry Kissinger

The former secretary of state probably regrets the celebrity given to his statement. He reminded us of the link between sex and power and of the role of that connection in the relationships of men and women in history. He may have been referring to the intoxicating attraction he had for women, but also perhaps, unknowingly, to how holding power could enlarge his personal sexual appetite.

It is a truism that males of any species are more aggressive than females. Men are thought to be shaped genetically toward aggression, but those genes, although conveying advantage for inclusive fitness, reflect the mutual shaping of both civilization and genetic mechanism (Macoby and Jacklin 1974). In a physiological oversimplification—yet one that carries a dominant social attitude—men sometimes mention the potential for violence residing in their gender; they comment with some wry pride that "testosterone is the most dangerous drug." Most men take the attribute of aggression as a fixed point for manhood, and some men want women to know of its potential for eruption, but as civilized men, they restrain it.[8]

Women also strive for personal achievement. But women are deeded a sturdier grasp on their womanhood. As contrasted with men, there is little testing of womanhood after adolescence brings it to a girl (Chodorow 1978). Girls and women are pulled by many needs and wishes, including in varying degrees, for example, concerns about status and appearance, but they are not driven in *the proof of themselves as women*, as men are in the proof of their manhood. Women are less disposed toward "pissing contests." A woman's strength is not as often tied to a struggle for womanhood.

When the need to murder children to hold power leads to indecisiveness, Lady Macbeth questions her husband provocatively, "Are you a man?" She thus asserts that the horrifying act should be obvious to a man; it is made more pointed because it comes from a woman. She *knows* what must be done; he lacks manhood because he cannot stand up to the horrific reality. A man acts, and she is saying that a man should be able to kill to get what he wants—for Macbeth and his lady, it is a kingdom.

Examples of women exerting effective counterforce are striking and rare. Ni-colo Machiavelli reported with awe that one remarkable woman, Countess Giro-lamo, caught in a conspiracy in which her husband was assassinated, deceived her captors by telling them that if allowed to go to the count's citadel, she would turn it over to them in return for her life and the lives of her "little ones." They kept her young children as hostages and allowed her to leave, certain she would return. The countess made her escape over the castle ramparts, reviling her ene-mies, and flung defiance at her attackers, who thought that holding her children would keep her to the coerced agreement: "And to convince them that she did not mind about her children, she exposed her sexual parts to them, and said that she was still capable of bearing more" (Machiavelli 1950, p. 487).[9]

Machiavelli used Girolamo to illustrate how nobility should act—to use force against force, to reverse fortune for victory, no matter what the cost. The count-ess soared above the role imposed on her, which dictated a mother's compliance for the sake of her children. From the traditional point of view, she gave up her motherhood and sacrificed that which has defined mothers—her focus on her children. She sacrificed motherhood for power and respect. She became the actor, the operant being, and demonstrated a potency greater than that of her captors; she met their force with her force, forced them into passivity and, by that, achieved a greater "nobility," that is, "manhood." She committed the strongest assault against the idea of mother and women; the woman abandoning her child receives the worst condemnation delivered by society. In her ability to renounce that basic tenet is a "nobility" of human action unfettered by the expected. Women are often honored as mothers, saints, or martyrs because of the passive sacrifice of self. A woman gets personal honor when she "acts like a man," *act-ing* courageously rather than accepting the fate ordained by men. Like the sol-diers, we are awed, appalled, admiring, and full of wonder.

SOCIAL ORDERING OF AGGRESSION

Male aggression against other men and women is more frequent than ag-gression carried out by women. Physical aggression by women is often viewed as abnormal, a breakout of the repressed.[10] Women in our society (and others) can be rejected by both men and women for being "aggressive females." Such des-ignation implies a deficit in the eyes of many, but not all, societies. An Australian aboriginal society supports and gives honor to fighting women. A field study by Victoria Burbank examined the aggressiveness of aboriginal women in one settlement she calls "Mangrove" and reported that these women physically fight with other women and with men, usually because of jealousy regarding men. Women in Mangrove manifest a full repertoire of aggressive acts—save murder. Men have the more serious weapons and the greater tendency to go to the physical extreme. The fighting women of Mangrove concede they cannot kill because they might cry and be sorry (Burbank 1994). But the community accords social parity for women's potential for aggression (Gough 1975).[11]

The view that aggressiveness is "natural" for men and "unnatural" for women derives more from cultural expectation than from innate female attributes. The threat of dangerous male violence teaches women caution, and there is also constant and real social restriction and castigation of female aggression in Western society. Because of the relative limitations imposed on women's aggression in our culture, even defiance is made to seem unnatural for women. The broad condemnation of physical aggression for women may truncate their ambitions in any field of endeavor, even those without obvious need for raw aggression. With aggression contained, a woman is more likely to be designated as a saint than a hero.

Researchers now find greater acceptance for women's physical aggression. Rather than solely promoting physical fighting for women (although that may be a result), such acceptance may help to untie women from a helpless position in any situation that requires assertive action.[12]

EPILOGUE

Every man thinks meanly of himself for not having been a soldier.
　　　　　　　—Samuel Johnson in April 10, 1778,
　　　　　　　letter to James Boswell, *Life of Johnson*

. . . The poignant misery of dawn begins to grow . . .
We only know that war lasts, rain soaks and clouds sag stormy.
Dawn massing in the east her melancholy army
Attacks once more in ranks on shivering ranks of gray.
　　　　　　　—Wilfred Owen, *Exposure*

I began this book to honor the former combatants in the Vietnam War whom I saw as psychiatric patients at the Boston Veterans Administration Hospital. As I've noted, because of public resentment toward the flawed war in which they had fought, they were not celebrated on their return to the United States, and this remains a part of their psychological damage. I wanted to bear witness for them.

The veterans told me of war's damage. But they also spoke of their discovery, in the midst of terror, of the absence from those social constraints felt before the war, of freedom, and of a wonder beyond anything they had previously experienced. I listened with interest, prompting more combat stories. The dialogue between doctor and veteran about combat's excitement was also meant to counter their sense of alienation from society. I did not and do not feel alien to them.

In the course of writing this book, I realized with a deepening conviction that I cannot assign human violence only to others. I know that the violence I write about is inside of me as well. Perhaps because of my acceptance of it, I did not find the veterans' excitement at war's wonders strange or incomprehensible. When I think about aggression, I start with my own.

I wanted to rouse the reader with the veterans' galvanizing narratives of combat, to put forward the awareness of the potential in all of us to feel that level of wonder and joy in the freedom found only in war. As I wrote the book, I had the thought that at the end I could say, "See, all men are made of the same stuff; we are all potential killers, and war unlocks that in the combatant. They are not to be faulted for their savage satisfaction or seen as less civilized than those who did not go to war." But that is far too simple.

I recognize that in my writing *about* combat's excitement, I have often used the voice familiar to me—somewhat distant from the galvanizing experiences expressed by veterans. They told it to me, and I presented it, but I also wrote *about* it. My writing is also ironic, the apposition of the incompatibility of combat with civilization. The satisfactions of destruction are counter to the idea of civilization I and others had come to view as normal and expectable in a world with little physical danger or certainly without the constant mortal danger of another person bent on killing. The veterans have been more aware of enemies who could not be influenced by argument until they were subdued; they certainly found that awareness in training and combat. They embraced war, felt that they were ready for it. Even with murderous rage toward their DI, they still had reason to thank him for their lives. That is generally true of war; they hated Vietnam but paradoxically still found in-country a greater reach of love than could otherwise have been realized.

I stepped back from the charged narratives to direct the book toward rational understanding of men's attachment to war. The idea of war, of soldiering, the essence of war, is an extension of a basic theme in the lives of growing boys—the absolute necessity to be a man in the eyes of other men. That is the early start of boys' attachment to war. In many cultures and nations, there is social support for the myth that soldiering is an expected means to unequivocal mastery and manhood. It is a social prescription, and it is a blueprint with the strongest moral imperative. Boys are to grow up seeking respect and identity with other boys in the assertion of their difference from girls. The socially enforced plan for boys demands that anyone who will call himself a man pass that initial test or else nervously expect that his peers will view him as a girl. These directives, preparation for war, are shaped by our society, which deeds boys more than girls the right to their aggression,[1] despite changed social attitudes about women in combat.

The blueprint for male aggression is a part of evolutionary adaptation. But culture, as much as genes, often determines boys' vector for competition. Boys are socially directed toward physical competence, eagerness for contest, and in such contest and in some circumstances are bent on winning and less afraid of personal harm—or even death—than of failing their comrades. This training does not produce a soldier, but it is the first step to a soldier's march.

A soldier's determination to kill or to subordinate enemy men and to protect his "brothers" is the center of combat morality. That can perforce exclude other moral views, such as justness of cause or concern about the humanity of the enemy. It is unusual for a soldier to resist the group pressure, although some soldiers take the risk. "So I'm on the fifties [50 mm machine guns] in a half track and my guys start shooting at a field where a farmer is plowing with his buffalo and his wife. He doesn't notice or acts like he doesn't. Then they begin to aim at him, the wife, . . . buffalo. I'm scared, but I'm really trying not to be noticed, and they tell me to open up also. What could I do?" (A.D.).

The beginnings of atrocity occur in ceding individual morality to the group. Love of comrades is compelling, and among friends brought together as a group for the purpose of violence, that love is often a prelude to immoral action. The idea can lead an entire nation away from the usual tenets of civilized behavior— to reach its apotheosis as it did, for example, in the Third Reich.

The history of the United States is often presented as being based on ambition and competition in which "winning is the only thing." In a related way, perhaps, the United States also has a long history of violence. We have an abundance of guns for the person who feels unequal to an opponent in the competition. We have become accustomed to the regularity of adults killing adults reported on the morning and evening news. Unusual killings can still grab our attention— serial murder; killing by children; or sniper attacks, such as those in 2002 when thirteen people in the Washington, D.C., area were murdered. Boys have murdered fellow students. Girls murder but less frequently. Social forces seem to be responsible. The rare person, constantly shamed by feeling a lack of respect may be less inclined toward more difficult self-examination than to the easy use of a gun that is readily available. However, he may believe a gun is a quick solution if the media and video games present killing as a means to dispel painful feelings of neglect and to achieve attention and respect. He may seize on the idea that there is a quick solution in a gun. Thus, killing rather than insight gets, albeit only temporarily, attention and respect.

To understand the psychological motivation for such murders, however, does not make the killing more acceptable. The negative effects of environment and other experiences are, in my view, only vaguely mitigating. They killed because that is what they wanted to do; they had the option of rejecting murder as the means to obtaining recognition and respect. Even if children with diminished self-esteem (perhaps because of social attitudes or other children's treatment of them) possess the urge to kill and have access to a gun, prohibitive laws force these children to reflect on alternatives. Even for the young, their obligation to civilization and to other human beings causes them not to act on these feelings.[2] "To understand" does not necessarily mean "to forgive."

Suicidal terrorists killed three thousand people in New York, Washington, D.C., and Pennsylvania on September 11, 2001, and suicidal attacks continue elsewhere in the world. We are not involved in a clash of civilizations (Huntington 1993). Our battle is not against the Islamic civilization; our present fight is against factions of that civilization. They adhere to a militant, terrorist redaction of the Koran. Islamic cults are hopelessly attached to reinterpretation of the words of the Prophet, with savage enmity toward others. The strength of fundamentalism is woven into it. They influence other Muslims and force them to follow their *jihad* (holy war, striving, sacred effort), bent on destruction of the West. There is a particular rage directed toward the United States, the "great Satan." They are aware of the decline of Arab dominance since the twelfth century and want to reestablish their Golden Age. They hold that the enmity and attack by the West has been responsible for their current situation. Although the crimes are on a different scale and differ in many ways, a common inciting factor of perceived disrespect toward them may provide the psychological underpinning to such murders. This has been the cause of many wars and a part of the continuing violence in the United States.

The human urge to destroy is kept inactive because it is etched in our minds in tandem with the extreme prohibition underscored by society's legal punishment of such acts and rigid structuring about when, by whom, and against whom it may be expressed. International law is also specific about killing. Islamists have unbound murder from its usual and expected prohibition by using God's command to sanctify it among themselves. They celebrate the death of their own children, as martyred in suicide attacks.

Not all situations are symmetrical, as in "They have their grievances, we have ours." Their intention is to attack repeatedly and subjugate us. They use the threat of future terrorism to keep us fearful and therefore to contract our expected options for free movement. If we do that, we would reduce our own freedom and approximate theirs. That makes all discussion about relative rightness irrelevant. Terrorists argue that they have no recourse, that the bullet and bomb are all that is available to the downtrodden. Whatever their desperation and motivation, we must fight back to defend our civilization and ourselves.

JOURNEY TO WAR

I have written of war's wonders and boys' early start toward soldiering. My idea in presenting the excitements of war, the near delirium in some nations at the start of war, contains an irony. The excitement of war, the emotional attachment to it, the boys available and often eager to fight it as ground soldiers are all in contrast to my own rational approach to life and a realistic approach to war that takes away the emotionally charged adornment of wonder, sex, and bonding of comrades and renders war as only grim, savage, and absurd in its tragic waste. The veterans' narratives of war resonated with me. I found a commonality in myself, and I hoped that the reader would feel some of the same. My initial purpose was to illustrate how we are all sadly, irrationally susceptible to the allure of war. I have not divested myself of a critical view of waging war; however, I am clear about the necessity of resolve and the seriousness of our struggle against struggle.

My attitude changed in the course of talking to veterans and writing this book. I began to see the world of combat as another kind of existence, a world with its own emotional attachments so strong that they could not be denied. I may have had the ability to fight in a war when I was young, but I cannot be certain that I had the required determination and endurance because I had not exposed myself to war's actuality, to the "test." I am aware now of how boyhood preparation for war is essential for national survival when the nation is attacked. The veterans reawakened a sense of my own ability to fight and endure. I felt some of that surge of strength, of ability at counterforce to attack that I felt as a young boy.

The September 2001 horror made clear the necessity for us, civilians, to be able to endure further attack. All of us must embrace the fact that we are at war and must be ready for future hurt and damage. People like me, professionals and academics who have led fairly protected lives, are often averse to physical risk and certainly to any war. Many of those I know have also rejected the idea of entering war for any reason, and they resist now facing the reality of continuing attack. Many of us are fearful that we may be unable to stand up to further attack if our community is attacked. In a related way, we have generally derogated combat soldiers—those who go to war unquestioningly when asked to go. There are times—now is one of them—when our civilization is attacked, and soldiers are the essential counterforce against the enemy. Those of us who have lived protected lives and avoided physical fighting (perhaps never were capable of it) now must be respectful and honor those who can. I am still against war but not every war.

We will defend our society with weapons but with the shared certainty that we will continue to examine ourselves. Democracies insist that the dignity of all humankind is vested in choice and in the liberty to dissent (Berlin 1969). Without that, a society cannot prevail, and a society that demeans women cannot win (Peters 2002).

PEACE AND WAR

What hope for peace can there be in such a turbulent and menacing context? With the social prescription for men to do battle, we are uncomfortably and paradoxically left with this searing question of whether peace is an attainable objective.

> War is "human nature at its highest dynamic . . . If [it] ever stopped we would have
> to reinvent it to redeem life from flat degeneration.
>
> —William James, *The Moral Equivalent of War*

William James was the most resonant voice at the beginning of the last century for permanently ending war; to that purpose, he illuminated the complex and deep attachment people felt toward war. He wrote feelingly of war as an excitement, an amusement, to stir the blood and to cleanse men of self-polluting concerns and to revitalize a nation, its economy, and its politics. There are good wars and not-so-good wars. Good wars start with a good reason—the best one is preservation of the nation and its citizens. That engenders unambiguous determination and often means victory—even against a powerful opponent. An "acceptable" war is for preservation of the nation's property and economic status, and the worst war is the adventure of the holding action, a war that proposes to draw a line against possible aggrandizement. The acceptable kind of war is best carried out with limited force and labor—cheaply—because the citizens of the nation do not want to spend a lot on a defective goal from the beginning. It is the national leader's task to present a full and ringing message about goals before starting a war.

The Moral Equivalent of War became a much-used phrase in antiwar movements in James's time. In the past hundred years, the phrase has not been used seriously, and the idea has become dated. Very few people would subscribe to the belief that we could find a substitute for war. James points to a constant internal emotional pressure for war, felt in the society and in the individual. He mirrors the compelling attachment to mortal conflict felt by all people. James described peacetime as a prelude to the disintegration of male ideals.

War and arguments against it are equally ancient. War is often compared to infection and plague; it grows as if from its own vital force. War devours (McNeil 1982). It is a terrible horseman riding with plague, drought, and hunger. Between the extremist arguments for war's virtues and those of the strongest pacifists for ending war forever is a third argument offered by those who can be called "realistic pacifists." That argument accepts the facts of history and an innate human ferocity, accepts war as always a potential part of the human condition, and suggests ways to delay its outbreak.

This third argument about war's inevitability holds the attention of most historians and commentators, many of whom are against war in principle. That is also the position, in only seeming paradox, of many professional soldiers. Indeed, there may be good argument for reserving the possibility of war fought for good cause. Contemporary elements of moral suasion can bend us toward a good, a necessary war. Lincoln emphasized the justness of the goal of the Civil War. In the height of that war's savagery and loss, he declared that he "hopes to God that it will not end until that attainment" (Ikle 1971, p. 1). As world commerce increased in the eighteenth and nineteenth centuries, a meliorist view predicted not only that its benefits to humankind would include greater abundance but also that personal interests focused on production and wealth would be strong enough to oppose any tendency to war. Thomas Paine stated in *The Rights of Man* that "commerce . . . permitted to act to the universal extent it is capable . . . would extirpate the system of war" (Paine 1791/1948, p. 209).

COMMON SENSE

In the nineteenth century, as part of such increased productivity, technological advance in the machines of war led to similar predictions. Long-range artillery, chemical weapons, and machine guns generated hope that war could no longer remain an option because it had become so massively destructive. The emergence of current weapons of mass destruction raised similar hopes at their birth, but these hopes have dimmed because the use of increasingly more efficient weapons and machines shows no sign of stopping.

WHY WAR?

> The present development of human beings requires, as it seems to me, no different explanation from that of animals.
>
> —Sigmund Freud, *Beyond the Pleasure Principle*

The possibility of stopping war by rational understanding of its attraction was suggested by Albert Einstein in a proposal to Sigmund Freud. The request from the great physicist to the great psychologist carried the urgency of the gathering threat to world peace and civilization in 1932. Einstein wrote of increasingly efficient technology in killing and the end of civilization in the war ahead. Both were aware that they were themselves contributors to and part of that civilization. Freud, however, criticized his own answer as "tedious and sterile," yet he could not shrink from responding to Einstein's request despite his apparent lack of interest in repeating what he had already sadly stated regarding human aggression (Moellenhoff and Moellenhoff 1978).[3] With little enthusiasm, Freud restated some of the aspects of his understanding of the crossed pulls of love and aggression. Our evolution dictated the use of force for survival; the instinctual satisfaction in killing for early humans in small groups is enhanced by technologically improved weapons, thus multiplying ancient savagery. Freud agreed with Einstein's statement that "man has within him a lust for hatred and destruction." He added that "conflicts of interest between men are settled by the use of violence. This is true of the whole animal kingdom from which men have no business excluding themselves." He offered the opinion that in human evolutionary history "killing an enemy satisfied an instinctual inclination." In a capitulation to war as deeded to us and inevitable, he finally asked [why we should not] "accept war as one of the many calamities of life."

Freud never successfully answered his own question but rather presented a confusing suggestion that war is "natural" and inherent to the evolving of culture, a process from which we benefit and suffer. He offered only the idea that the reason he and others like him are against war is because pacifists have a *constitutional* intolerance of it. Freud confounded individual aggression and the far more complex expression of national aggression through highly technical modern warfare. The level of organization nations require for war is qualitatively different from the rage that follows an individual attack. Of course, accepting the notion of war as natural does not mean that it must inevitably lead to the full outbreak of hostilities (Einstein and Freud 1933).

AN EVOLUTIONARY PERSPECTIVE

A tool in hand defined and separated the earliest humans from common roots with apes (Wilson 1975). Although we did not enter the world as soldiers, hominid humans certainly came as predators and killed animals and other humans with weapons as tools (O'Connell 1989). Members of other species—apes, for example—kill their own kind, but they do it less often, with far less ability at communication and organization, and far less massively.

Twenty-first-century soldiers are not ice age warriors. They have been shaped by the social context in which they grew up and by their sense of themselves as men. They are forced in peace to live out a fearful contradiction—they have been forced to kill by the society and nation that prohibits it (Grossman 1995).

The moral and legal position about men at war is clear: mortal action against unarmed civilians is always murder, and there is no expiation for the crime. Command has primary responsibility for preventing murder by the soldiers they have trained and set loose as a mortal force. The difficulty of living with that antinomy argues for its urgency, not for its abandonment.

The technological evolution of the machines of war escalated in Europe in the sixteenth century, and war became increasingly efficient in the number of casualties produced (McNeil 1982). We detest war because of its destructiveness but simultaneously promote it, possibly because skill at war was the major difference between hominids and apes.

There is evidence that the dawn of hominids and the increasing ascendancy of our species began with an emergent ability of some primates to conduct organized combat. Those apes with a superior organizational ability were the primordial humans, and by that adaptive quality, they differentiated themselves from our very close cousins, the chimpanzees (with whom we share 98.6% of our genetic material). Such organizational capacities furthered both material abundance and dominance of groups of warrior apes (or ape-men), who not only hunted but also created a warrior culture that supported predation and the raiding of other hominids (Bigelow 1969).

In this view, war exerted the strongest evolutionary pressures over the eons. The attributes for survival in war honed the edge of human thinking, furthered language for communication and deception, shaping human feeling and behavior generationally. Hominids adjacent to groups of other marauding human predators could survive only if they responded effectively against attacks from others by developing organization, communication, aggressiveness, and greater efficiency in killing. To adapt efficiently, they developed strong emotional attachments to those within the group and produced both prosperity and the dominance of the human species over time. Given the usual time scale for species change, war propelled us in a relatively short time toward the evolution of those mental capacities that make for perpetual and successful war. Our civilization, it is said, evolved from such "dawn warriors" (Bigelow 1969).

Aggression between groups may have its primordial beginnings in the Pleistocene, but war, as we know it, is far more complex, so complex as to be qualitatively different from primordial raiding. War now involves the political, sensed or real danger to a nation, its people, and its ethos, the preservation and extension of boundaries.

IS WAR INESCAPABLE?

> Yet the poor fellows think they are safe! They think that the war is over! Only the dead have seen the end of war.   —George Santayana, Soliloquy #25: "Tipperary"

In Plato's time, every city-state was at perpetual war with every other city-state. Odysseus declared in the *Iliad:* "The men whom Zeus decrees, from youth to old age / must wind down our brutal wars to the bitter end until we drop and die, down to the last man" (Homer 1990, 14.105–7).

> They shall beat their swords into plowshares, and their spears into pruning hooks: nation shall not lift up sword against nation, neither shall they learn war any more.
>
> —Isaiah 2:4; Micah 4:3

With all that I have learned from my experience with courageous Vietnam soldiers, I sadly conclude that strong nations must use their strength to monitor the justness of war, in its inception and its conduct under the rule of law. War will continue to shape men into "killers" who otherwise would have lived out their lives without violence. That releases no one from constraint against evil in war. We will have to make war, but we do not have to become killers. As individuals or a nation, we cannot seek moral refuge for uncivilized acts in the belief that we have no escape from brains that are a million years old.

We should know what to expect and to be prepared for the probability of civilian casualties. Americans can absorb damage; our enemies cannot kill all of us. We can go forward with the moral will to avoid war and to endure for our part of civilization and for each other.

That we must wage war for civilization is clear; it seems we must fight and kill for our self-preservation. The veterans made me realize that I could still feel the rage available to kill those who came to kill me and mine. Now I see the available rage as necessary for maintaining our own civilization. The events of September 11, 2001, underscored that. We persist as a nation and as a civilization only because we have often fought mortal battles for our preservation. Our arts, laws, and science as part of our civilization continue, not because of their many virtues, but because we also have the moral will to defend them—and now the battle is against a fundamentalist faction of Islam whose unshakeable dogma is restriction without debate, intolerance, and the demeaning of women.

> Older men declare war. But it is youth that must fight and die.
> And it is youth who must inherit the tribulation, the sorrow,
> and the triumphs that are the aftermath of war.
>
> —Herbert Hoover, address to the twenty-third Republican National Convention

NOTES

1. Gerhoch of Reichersberg in the twelfth century defined the four elements constituting all "play" or "game" as "imitation (of others), or mimesis—as in the theater; conflict; endurance and hazard." He believed that all these attributes of human play were related to the "game of love" (Cox 1993). There was no reference to war, but men who have been at war would have no problem with the seeming contradictoriness of mortal contest in conjunction with "game," "play," and "love."

2. The salaries of professional athletes have been examined in terms of the "social good" they bring.

3. It is a mild surprise to find out that, in the saliva of spectators watching the World Cup, there was a more than 25 percent increase in testosterone levels in supporters of the victorious Brazilians watching the match on television mirrored by a matching decrease in testosterone levels of the losing fans (Fielden, Lutter, and Dabbs 1994). It is important to remember that there is greater complexity to the neurophysiology of dominance than is reflected in shifts in any individual hormones or specific neurotransmitters. Serotonin also varies with social dominance and competence and is also increased by the relatively new group of prescribed antidepressants, such as Prozac (Masters and McGuire 1993). All are mutually interactive by mechanisms that are not understood.

4. Rock stars and other entertainers are also celebrated because of the risks of being criticized, disliked, and discarded by fans with whom the relationship, like that of every fan (meaning "fanatic"), is ambivalent. Fans have the power to bring down the adored if they are displeased. In the case of popular entertainers, the competition is for the fans' support.

5. Their dread of father is "less uncanny in quality." It is attached to physical punishment and perhaps to a fantasized attack that removes manhood. But there is also fear of absolute disapproval or rejection—the shame of judgment about achieving necessary manhood.

6. The men and women protesting the Vietnam War often wore military surplus clothing, but not in the manner ordered by regulation. Such clothing gave them an aura of strong purpose and a bonding with others. Their mission took on urgency. Stopping the war required bonding, force, and a willingness to endure privation and attack—that may be the reason for the borrowed uniforms.

A Vietnam veteran said, "I couldn't stand them (the peace movement protestors). I hated them—but I thought, looking at them up against the police and the military 'they are all alone . . . Christ they have balls.' I could never go up against the Corps—I wanted to, a lot—maybe still do" (E.P.).

7. Chagnon's work has been severely criticized more recently. Tierney (2002) questions Chagnon's anthropology as well as the lack of objectivity of his critics.

8. In some societies, all boys' initiation into manhood is brought about as a symbolic birth. Boys are symbolically born by, or through, men in a ritual meant to mimic child-birth—the *couvade*. The men do this, they say, with the "magic stolen from women." By means of this symbolic ritual of birth, men play out the birth of a boy by, or through, a man, thus making him into a man. Men also forcibly keep women away from observing *couvade* because they say it might let the women take back the stolen magic; more than likely, they avoid ridicule regarding their lack of women's real power.

9. Dr. Jarl Jorstad described, "some numbers of us died of disease and starvation before our rescue by a train of ambulances from the Swedish and Danish Red Cross, led by Count Folke-Bernadotte of Sweden. We all arrived, Norwegian and similar Danish former students in the resistance on May 1, 1945, one week before Germany capitulated" (Jarl Jorstad, personal communication).

10. Such views were further amplified by Goebbels and compared with iconography by Speer as adornment to promote mystic race and *ur* myths as history (Speer 1976; Sereny 1996). Gabriele d'Annunzio did the same for Italian fascism at the turn of the century (Woodhouse 1998). The goal of subjugation of others substituted for any textured political purpose.

11. In defense of the biological given, at least among primitive peoples, there is fitness utility in restricting the number of women and having the strongest males produce the most progeny as a result (Harris 1984). The population is less than if there were enough women available for reproduction so that all males had a chance at reproduction. Population growth is also checked by the higher mortality rate for the *Unokai*, the warriors who risk their own death in predatory raids with greatest frequency. The *Unokai*, however, out-produce the non-*Unokai* by a ratio 5:1 (Chagnon 1983).

12. Military cadre rely on the coercive power of males in groups for promoting group aggression. Training taps into anxiety about test of manhood—"the idea of war." Once set in motion, risk of life and killing may be loved by a only few, but most other boys will do it out of necessity, out of the shame of not doing it, the fear of failure, and to win the approval of men.

13. All the tribal groups that engage in warfare against other groups and also in violent warlike activity and physically aggressive games within the tribe, have rules of separation of boys from their mothers and from girls; older men raise boys through adolescence and indoctrination into manhood. Such rules are often vigorously reinforced by tradition and/or religious doctrine.

14. German militarists emphasized training for boys that enforced separation from

women and excluded contact with their mothers (Waite 1952; Craig 1982). In any culture in which there is absolute separation of sexes, there is an expectation of increased male aggressiveness.

TWO   BROTHERS AND COMRADES

1. There is also decreased self-awareness and decreased self-monitoring (Diener 1980). The deindividuated may feel shamed and contrite only with facing strong external authority after violation of the expected social rules governing individual behavior.

2. As part of the negative feeling at home against the Vietnam War, there was severe criticism of all the military, and they were blamed for the war and its continuation. The national ethos and civilized values were undermined by the war. Marine training was said to inculcate perverse values and exchange for a "bogus manhood." The environment of combat training was characterized as a brutalizing, sadistic system directed at destroying individualism by calculated sadism and identification with the brutal DI.

THREE   KILLING

1. Most of the killing in modern war is launched at a distance from the target. Soldiers who kill and who die are most often hidden or are beyond the range of one another. Since cannon entered war, artillerymen have inflicted the greatest numbers of casualties (up to 60 percent) with the least vulnerability to themselves (Dunnigan 1988, p. 492). Since World War II, infantrymen's personal weapons have acquired greater range, are smaller and lighter, allowing a soldier to fire *toward* if not *at* the enemy while keeping relatively unexposed. David Grossman points to the increasing ease and loss of the restraint to kill as technology puts greater distance between the shooter and the target.

2. The M-16A used initially in Vietnam was notorious for jamming and was replaced.

3. General Lee, in command of the well-positioned Confederate Army, was looking down at the Potomac River and contemplating the imminent destruction of the Union forces (Ward, Burns, and Burns 1990).

4. The bayonet is rarely used in combat as the knife at the end of a rifle but more usually for "domestic chores."

FOUR   KILLERS

1. Downs agreed to be interviewed for this book, although he had some concern about its potential antiwar bias.

2. V.E. referred to John Hathcock, a well-known Marine who was responsible for combat innovations (reported in Henderson 1986).

3. Shakespeare presents a French knight, sensing imminent defeat at Agincourt, sees a possible retrieval of honor in a desperate and terrible act that is against the rules of war;

he invades the English camp to terrify and disrupt. He kills unarmed boy servants. He starts out knowing that what he is about to do is very wrong and simultaneously sees it as necessary. He also wishes his own death for the evil he is about to commit: "Let life be short, else shame will be too long" (Shakespeare, *Henry V,* act 4, scene 6). Guilt, according to one commentator, allows continued killing, as if guilt expiates the person to do more killing. Guilt attaches the killer to society and comforts the breaker of sacrament by reminding him of the connection to community moral norms (Bourke 1999). A more easily accepted concept is that guilt does not in itself expiate the killer in order to allow him to do more, but that in war, society allows a "guilty ecstasy," superego control reduced for the soldier by socially sanctioned aggression (Ehrenreich 1997).

4. The truth or falsity of such stories is not the sole basis for interest. Many of these stories are constructed from events glimpsed and for propaganda against enemies. But the fact that they are conceivable and believable informs us of the degree of insentience that can occur with possession of overwhelming power.

5. The idea of the "dawn warrior" has been called "absurd" by one critic in a brief redaction of Bigelow's guess that war promoted cooperation and shaped us as a species (Gorney 1971). War may have shaped us, but language and civilization have shaped war. Dawn warriors did not make "war" as we know it. They engaged in predatory raiding, still found as the center of preindustrial social groups such as the Unamamo (Chagnon 1988) and the Jivaro (Harner 1984). Chimpanzees observed in the wild also form "war" parties, raid and kill chimps living in groups other than their own (Bigelow 1969; Wilson 1978; Wrangham and Peterson 1996).

Individual predispositions certainly evolve out of the general tendency of men to be aggressive; it is a fitness attribute shaped by evolution. War and increased technical efficiency in delivering death to an enemy seems only to supplement that of our basic aggressive nature. But if Pleistocene hominids routinely turned aggressive against others within their "blood-related" group, without restraint, and killed for individual sustenance and sex, that would have disrupted the group's cohesiveness and decidedly decreased the group's chances for survival. Restraint against aggression and altruism is also endorsed by DNA; it is reasonable to assume that it is also "factory installed" and constantly shapes behavior as a part of Darwinian inclusive fitness (Hamilton 1964; Kofoed and Macmillan 1989).

SIX DAMAGE

1. Although the long-term consequences of psychological stressors have been noted from the beginning of modern psychiatry, the focus for psychiatrists after World War I in Europe and the United States turned toward the examination of *inner* psychological conflict and the repression of wish as the source of "neurotic suffering." "Real" rather than "imagined" psychological trauma as the initiator of enduring psychological difficulty was often disregarded until the psychic aftermath of the Vietnam War unfolded. Veterans came back from that war with symptoms recognized as existing in a civilian population as well,

and a general category of posttraumatic stress disorder replaced the designation of Vietnam combat syndrome applied exclusively to those veterans. Psychiatrists and psychologists began to recognize that former combatants in Vietnam were returning with psychological symptoms directly traceable to their war experiences. The Vietnam War reawakened interest in "real trauma"—that is, events that actually happened, as opposed to the almost exclusive interest in analyzing "imagined psychological trauma" that had been a dominant and continuing psychoanalytic approach for the relief of "neurotic suffering." Since the Vietnam War, there has been a widening interest among mental health care professionals in identifying traumatic events and in tracing their effect on human adaptation. Psychological trauma has been indicted as contributing to the development of many psychological problems, including ineffectiveness in managing stress and relationships, depression, cognitive deficits, dissociative states, multiple personality, and anxiety.

2. During World War I, an antiwar group reportedly sent the same leaflets to both sides proclaiming in English and in German: "Shoot all the officers and go home."

SEVEN   MYTHS AND PERCEPTIONS

1. The War was and is generally accepted by the British as a moral necessity (Fussell 1975). Niall Fergueson, among others (John Keegan), concluded that World War I did not need to happen, and if Britain had not deemed it necessary to enter a conflict, all would have worked out better for the populations then and for the future, and World War II would have been avoided as well.

EIGHT   THE WONDER OF WAR

1. In the face of the wondrous, what we unthinkingly accept as our daily reality is but an anesthetic. In severe competitive tests, soldiers find the most wonder and life. The experience of wonder creates major changes in perception, purpose, and meaning that cannot be equaled in peace. The comparison can lead to despondency and a strong sense of loss. War's urgency and wonder annihilate usual meaning, freeing a young soldier from strongly held ideas about what is "right." Peacetime attitudes and morality have no relevance to the most important issue in combat—survival and care for comrades, often called "brothers." Only survival has meaning limited to friends and self. War strips away complex moral values and concerns, offering instead a dreadful freedom. Reality—what is perceived as real—most often resides in the severest experience, adversity, and contest. The quotidian is pale compared with that and less real because it is less vibrant, less attached to emotional force.

2. The initial meaning of *berserk* in Norse refers to the bearskin worn as protection in combat. *Berserk* means without the bearskin.

TEN WOMEN AND WAR

1. Part of the evidence is a record from 1330 at Windsor Castle noting the possession of a large weapon called "Domina Gunilda," and because there was no record of a distinguished lady named Gunilda in or near Windsor, it is assumed that the fourteenth-century designation had been handed down from Scandinavian times. Cf. *Oxford English Dictionary* under "gun." In more modern times (with ordnance), the weapons bearing death are named for women, the missiles the weapons deliver are male. The atomic bomb carried by Enola Gay to Hiroshima was called "Little Boy."

2. Men have historically controlled the reproductive capacity of women. Anthropologists have observed the predatory raiding behavior of prestate peoples, such as the approximately fifteen thousand Yanomamo who live in the forests of Brazil and neighboring areas of Venezuela. They have concluded that the evolutionary adaptive force is primary in shaping this central behavior (Chagnon 1983).

Although the warrior himself echoes a Darwinian motivation for raiding, the exclusively adaptationist conclusion is strongly debated. One fact not in favor of absolute Darwinism is that the Yanomamo regularly kill and neglect girl infants—counter to the promotion of reproductive access and counteradaptivity.

3. The primal competition among small cells was for access to the largest ones, which contained a rich supply of nutrients within their cell walls. While a group of cells gathered food for their own individual reproduction, a group of smaller cells, differing because they were smaller and quicker—because they "traveled light," stored only enough nutrition for motile sorties to "hijack" the larger cells. They competed among themselves for the plunder of those stockpiling organisms.

There are social scientists who present the basic design of the template for dominance as originating in historical accident and social custom, rather than Nature. But others point out that dominance between and within groups of early humans has always been based on physical strength and size, and there is strong logic to the idea that men's continuing domination over women also springs from that aspect of Nature. Further unequal access to women and reproduction is the basic condition of men in primitive human societies; the position of dominance depends on size and strength. Males who can successfully overcome other males, or at least bluff them into believing that they can, have access to females in widely varying animal species. This has been a pretext for war since Homer's time. When enemy males in prenation tribes were all killed, and the only survivors of the war were the women given as slaves to the victors, such women were made alien; they were viewed as part of the hated enemy (Ehrenreich 1997).

4. That is also observed by anthropologists among primates, particularly the bonobo (misnamed "pygmy" chimpanzees) who possess physical and temperamental characteristics similar to humans. Reconciliation typically occurs with sexual union (De Waal 1989).

5. The Articles of War prescribe similar punishment for rape as for murder (Morris 1996). Judges in a court-martial, however, often have difficulty in finding rape as equiva-

lent to murder for combatants, and sometimes they let soldiers who have raped go free. (Morris 1996).

6. Regulations against violent crimes among military personnel are effective in peacetime. From 1987 to 1992, the rates of murder and incidence of aggravated assault were lower in the military than among civilians, and this is true of rape as well as other violent crimes.

7. The Defense Advisory Committee on Women in the Service (DACOWITS) was set up in 1951 to help recruit women as auxiliaries in the Korean War. Those of us in the armed services in that era were aware of the appearance of small-sized noncom (noncommissioned officer) stripes and of a mandated attitude toward accepting women equal in rank really as equal. The military made standards of training for women less rigorous with regard to physical stamina and strength. There was resentment at all levels regarding standards. Command, caught between their fear that DACOWITS would interfere with promotions and the wish to keep the military at a standard of focused aggressiveness, has instituted sensitivity training and sexual harassment programs (McDougall 1997). Still there have been revelations of widespread harassment of female soldiers on all, including the highest, levels. There have been increasing scrutiny and regulations on male soldiers' sexual conduct and severest penalties for unwanted sexual approach, with possible dishonorable discharge even for those of the highest rank.

8. The statement about testosterone is physiologically inaccurate: In young men where testosterone is acutely, profoundly, and transiently lowered artificially, a significant *increase* in aggression is noted (Bagatell et al. 1994). Even the expression of raw aggression is determined by complex factors and testosterone level is only part of the story.

9. "E per mostrare che de' suoi figliuoli non si curarra, mostro' loro le membra genitali, dicendo che aveva ancora il modo di rifarne" (Nicolo Machiavelli, speech from the First Decade of Tito Livio).

10. There has been then a general view that women may engage in aggressive acts but stop short of killing. There are an estimated five hundred serial killers of both sexes, at large and unidentified. These are the *"crème de la crème*, of murderers, the ultimate challenge to authority." The United States has an astonishing 75 percent of the world's serial killers within 5 percent of the world's population (Norris 1988). Male serial murderers receive great attention.

Women do, indeed, murder, and there are many women who have been serial killers. One estimate is one hundred since 1900 (Kelleher and Kelleher 1998). But, they are popularly viewed as rarities, so outside of the general pattern as to be ignored. That has stimulated some writers to object (Pearson 1997; Kelleher and Kelleher 1998). The objection is about a familiar inequity in acknowledgment. In forcing women into an ultimately nonaggressive position as nurturer, caretaker, and domestic angel, some see and object to the negation of women's full range of passion. Some feminists would assert a claim to notoriety denied—including the ability to be an ultimately aggressive challenge to authority. There is a confounding statistic regarding murder of one intimate partner by another among African Americans; in the last thirty years in Chicago in this population, women, not men, killed their partners with two times the frequency (Pearson 1997).

11. Kathleen Gough indicated that in tribal societies men control weapons, giving them the control of ultimate force. Where there is war, boys are preferred and are raised as aggressive warriors. The male advantage in establishing monopoly over weapons is so that war is the exclusive prerogative of males and therefore sex can be a principle reinforcement for fierce behavior involving mortal risk.

12. Male and female sports fans follow professional women boxers. Athletic events that involve body contact have not been of interest to women—or spectators—until recently. Women's soccer was a closely followed Olympic event.

EPILOGUE

The complete quotation of the Samuel Johnson epigraph includes sailors, who, in Johnson's time, suffered greatest rigors in bringing home the catch. Johnson said that gentlemen in London, ordering fish in a restaurant, would be in awe if they knew what privation and risk it took to bring the fish to table. Commercial fishing is still one of the most dangerous ways of earning a living.

1. That is not a statement to which all biologists would subscribe—there are many biologists who place adaptation as primary—the process by which genetic material is selected for its ability to survive. The gene has an executive function, in that view, making us what we are, body and soul (Wilson 1975). That extreme view of genetic determinism is not as loud as it was when E. O. Wilson set forth his idea of sociobiology—outlining with examples how what we are is derived from adaptation and "fitness"—meaning that those genes that survive to be reiterated in future generations are the ones that helped the organism to reproduce successfully in its particular environment.

2. There are mental health professionals who sincerely believe that discovered deficiencies in rearing excuse all kinds of the most unsocial behavior—even murder.

3. The brief exchange between two of the great illuminating intellects of the twentieth century was published as *Why War?* (Einstein and Freud 1933)

REFERENCES

American Psychiatric Association. 2000. *Desk Reference to the Diagnostic Criteria from DSM-IV-TR*, 218–21. Washington, D.C.: American Psychiatric Association.

Atwood, M. 1972. *Surfacing*. London: Virago Press.

Bacon, F. 1996. Of the true greatness of kingdoms and estates. In *A Critical Edition of the Major Works of Francis Bacon*, ed. B. Vickers, 397–403. New York: Oxford University Press.

Bagatell, C. J., J. A. Heiman, J. E. Rivier, and W. J. Bremner. 1994. Effects of endogenous testosterone and estradiol in sexual behavior in normal young men. *Journal of Clinical Endocrinology* 78 (2): 711–16.

Balint, M. 1939. Critical notes on theory of pregenital organizations of the libido. In *Primary Love and Psychoanalytic Technique*, ed. M. Balint, 37–58. New York: Liveright.

Barker, P. 1996. *The Ghost Road*. New York: Plume/Penguin.

Barnes, E. 1994. A sniper's tale. *Time*, March 14.

Bataille, G. 1986. *Erotism, Death and Sensuality*. San Francisco: City Lights.

Berlin, I. 1969. *Four Essays on Liberty*. Oxford: Oxford University Press; berlin.wolf.ox.ac.uk /lists/bibliography/onepagebiblio.html, accessed September 15, 2004.

Betzig, L. 1986. *Despotism and Differential Reproduction*. New York: Aldine de Gruyter.

Bigelow, R. S. 1969. *The Dawn Warriors: Man's Evolution towards Peace*. Boston: Little, Brown.

Bilton, M., and K. Sim. 1992. *Four Hours in My Lai: A War Crime and Its Aftermath*. London: Viking.

Bond, B. 1986. *War and Society in Europe, 1870–1970*. New York: Oxford University Press.

Boswell, J. 1998. *Life of Johnson*. Repr. Oxford: Oxford University Press, 1904.

Bourke, J. 1999. *An Intimate History of Killing*. New York: Basic Books.

Boyd, W. Y. 1994. *The Gentle Infantryman*. Los Angeles: Burning Gate Press.

Bradshaw, S. L., C. D. Ohlde, and J. B. Hjorne. 1991. The love of war: Vietnam and the traumatized veteran. *Bulletin of the Menninger Clinic* 55:96–103.

Bremner, J. D., S. Southwick, E. Brett, A. Fontana, R. Rosenheck, and D. S. Charney. 1992. Dissociation and posttraumatic stress disorder in Vietnam combat veterans. *American Journal of Psychiatry* 149:328–32.

Browning, C. 1992. *Ordinary Men: Reserve Police Battalion 101 and the Final Solution in Poland*. New York: HarperCollins.

Brownmiller, S. 1975. *Against Our Will: Men, Women, and Rape*. New York: Simon & Schuster.

Broyles, W., Jr. 1984. Why men love war. *Esquire*, November, pp. 55–65.

Buford, B. 1993. *Among the Thugs.* New York: Vintage.

Burbank, V. K. 1994. *Fighting Women: Anger and Aggression in Aboriginal Australia.* Berkeley: University of California Press.

Buruma, I. 1994. *The Wages of Guilt.* New York: Farrar, Strauss & Giroux.

Byers, J. T. 2003. The things they wrote: The final letters written by U.S. soldiers recently killed in Iraq. *New York Times,* November 11.

Campbell, J. 1968. *The Masks of God: Creative Mythology.* New York: Viking Press.

Capps, W. H. 1991. *The Vietnam Reader.* New York: Routledge.

Caputo, P. 1977. *A Rumor of War.* New York: Ballantine.

Chagnon, N. 1983. *Yanomamo: The Fierce People,* 3rd ed. New York: Holt, Rinehart & Winston.

Chagnon, N. 1988. Life histories, blood revenge and warfare in a tribal population. *Science* 239:985–92.

Chodorow, N. 1978. *The Reproduction of Mothering.* Berkeley: University of California Press.

Churchill, W. 1940. Speech to the House of Commons following the Battle of Dunkirk, June 4.

Churchill, W. 1941. Speech to the public on BBC, July 14.

Churchill, W. 1949. Introd. to *The Secret Battle,* by A. P. Herbert. New York: Oxford University Press.

Clausewitz, C. 1984. *On War.* Trans. and ed. M. Howard and P. Paret. Princeton, N.J.: Princeton University Press.

Conroy, P. 1980. *The Lords of Discipline.* Boston: Houghton Mifflin.

Cox, M. 1993. *The Group as Poetic Play-Ground.* The 1990 Foulkes Annual Lecture. London: Jessica Kingsley. Audiotape.

Craig, G. 1982. *The Germans.* New York: Putnam.

Csikszentmihalyi, M. 1991. *Flow: The Psychology of Optimal Experience.* New York: Harper-Collins.

Czerny's International Auction House. 2004. *Armi Antiche, Armature e Militaria: Sarzana, 22 e 23 Maggio 2004* (Sarzana: Czerny's 2004), nos. 204–209: 18–19c (daggers with erotic themes).

Daly, M., and M. I. Wilson. 1988. *Homicide.* Hawthorne, N.Y.: Aldine de Gruyter.

Dawkins, R. 1972. *The Selfish Gene.* Oxford: Oxford University Press.

De Beauvoir, S. 1970. *The Second Sex.* New York: Knopf.

Dentan, R. K. 1968. *The Semai, a Nonviolent People of Malaysia.* New York: Holt, Rinehart & Winston.

DeParle, J. 1995. The man inside Bill Clinton's foreign policy. *New York Times Magazine,* August 20.

DeWaal, F. 1989. *Peacemaking among Primates.* Cambridge, Mass.: Harvard University Press.

Diener, E. 1980. Deindividuation: The absence of self awareness and self regulation in group members. In *Psychology of Group Influence,* ed. P. B. Paulus, 209–42. Hillsdale, N.J.: Lawrence Erlbaum.

Dixon, N. F. 1976. *On the Psychology of Military Incompetence.* London: Jonathan Cape.

Draper, T. 1995. McNamara's peace. *New York Review of Books,* May 11.

Dunnigan, J. F. 1988. *How to Make War.* New York: William Morrow.

Dyan, M. 1997. Boys want guns. *Forbes,* January 27.

Dyer, G. 1985. *War.* New York: Crown.

Ehrenreich, B. 1997. *Blood Rites: Origins and History of the Passions of War.* New York: Holt.

Einstein, A., and S. Freud. 1933. *Why War?* International Institute of Intellectual Co-operation. Paris: League of Nations.

Eliot, T. S. 1967. Burnt Norton (no. 1 of *Four Quartets*). In *The Complete Poems and Plays of T. S. Eliot,* 191–98. London: Faber & Faber.

Eliot, T. S. 1967. Little Gidding (no. 4 of *Four Quartets*). In *The Complete Poems and Plays of T. S. Eliot,* 191–98. London: Faber & Faber.

Ezrahi, Y. 1997. *Rubber Bullets: Power and Conscience in Modern Israel.* New York: Farrar, Straus & Giroux.

Faludi, S. 1994. The naked citadel. *New Yorker,* September 5.

Farnsworth, E., director and producer. 1990. *Thanh's War* (documentary). PBS, San Francisco KQED. Berkeley: University of California.

Fenton, J. 1996. Goodbye to all that. *New York Review of Books,* June 20, pp. 59–64.

Fergueson, N. 1999. *The Pity of War: Explaining World War I.* New York: Basic Books.

Festinger, L., A. Pepitone, and T. Newcomb. 1952. Some consequences of deindividuation in a group. *Abnormal and Social Psychology* 47:382–89.

Fielden, J., C. Lutter, and J. Dabbs. 1994. *Basking in Glory: Testosterone Changes in World Cup Soccer Fans.* Atlanta: Psychology Department, Georgia State University.

French, M. 1992. *The War against Women.* London: Hamish Hamilton.

Freud, S. 1959a. Beyond the pleasure principle. In Vol. 18 of *The Standard Edition of the Complete Psychological Works of Sigmund Freud,* 7–64. Trans. J. Strachey. London: Hogarth Press.

Freud, S. 1959b. Three essays on sexuality. In Vol. 7 of *The Standard Edition of the Complete Psychological Works of Sigmund Freud,* 125–243. Trans. J. Strachey. London: Hogarth Press.

Fritz, S. G. 1995. *Frontsoldaten: The German Soldier in World War II.* Lexington: University Press of Kentucky.

Fussell, P. 1975. *The Great War and Modern Memory.* London: Oxford University Press.

Fussell, P. 1989. *Wartime: Understanding and Behavior in the Second World War.* New York: Oxford University Press.

Geyl, P. 1986. *Napoleon, For and Against.* Harmondsworth, Middlesex, UK: Penguin Books.

Gibson, J. 1994. *Warrior Dreams: Paramilitary Culture in Post Vietnam America.* New York: Hill and Wang.

Gilligan, J. 1996. *Violence: Our Deadly Epidemic and Its Causes.* New York: Putnam.

Gilmore, D. 1990. *Manhood in the Making: Cultural Concepts of Masculinity.* New Haven, Conn.: Yale University Press.

Goldhagen, D. 1997. *Hitler's Willing Executioners.* New York: Vintage Books.

Golding, W. 1954. *The Lord of the Flies.* London: Faber & Faber.

Gorney, R. 1971. Interpersonal intensity, competition, and synergy: Determinants of achievement, aggression, and mental illness. *American Journal of Psychiatry* 128 (4): 436–45.

Gough, K. 1975. The origin of the family. In *Toward an Anthropology of Women,* ed. R. Reiter, 51–76. New York: Monthly Review Press.

Gray, J. G. 1970. *The Warriors: Reflections on Men in Battle.* New York: Harper & Row.

Green, B., M. C. Grace, J. D. Lindy, G. C. Gleser, and A. Leonard. 1990. Risk factors for PTSD and other diagnoses in a general sample of Vietnam veterans. *American Journal of Psychiatry* 147:729–73.

Grimsley, M. 1995. *The Hard Hand of War: Union Military Policy toward Southern Civilians, 1861–1865.* New York: Cambridge University Press.

Grossman, D. 1995. *On Killing: The Psychological Cost of Learning to Kill in War and Society.* Boston: Little, Brown.

Gullace, N. F. 1997. White feathers and wounded men: Female patriotism and the memory of the Great War. *Journal of British Studies* 36 (April): 178–206.

Gutmann, S. 1997. Sex and the soldier. *New Republic,* February 24.

Hamilton, W. D. 1964. The genetical evolution of social behavior. *Journal of Theoretical Biology* 7:116.

Hanson, V. D. 2001. *Carnage and Culture: Landmark Battles in the Rise of Western Power.* New York: Doubleday.

Harner, M. J. 1984. *Jívaro, People of the Sacred Waterfalls.* Berkley: University of California Press.

Harries, M., and S. Harries. 1991. *Soldiers of the Sun.* New York: Random House.

Harris, M. 1984. A cultural materialist theory of ban and village warfare: The Yanomamo test. In *Warfare, Culture and Environment,* ed. R. B. Fergusen. Orlando, Fla.: Academic Press.

Heinrich, W. 1956. *The Cross of Iron.* Trans. R. Winston and C. Winston. Indianapolis: Bobbs-Merrill.

Helprin, M. 1991. *A Soldier of the Great War.* New York: Harcourt Brace Jovanovich.

Henderson, C. 1986. *Marine Sniper.* New York: Berkley.

Herman, J. L. 1991. *Trauma and Recovery.* New York: Basic Books.

Herr, M. 1991. *Dispatches.* New York: Basic Books.

Hersh, S. M. 2004. Chain of command: How the Department of Defense mishandled the disaster at Abu Ghraib. *New Yorker,* May 17.

Holmes, O. W. 1914/2000. Bread and the newspaper. In *The Oxford Book of American Essays,* ed. B. Matthews, 114–29. Oxford: Oxford University Press. Repr. Bartleby.com.

Holmes, R. 1989. *Acts of War.* New York: Free Press.

Homer. 1961. *The Iliad.* Trans. O. Lattimore. Chicago: University of Chicago Press.

Homer. 1990. *The Iliad.* Trans. R. Fagles. New York: Penguin.

Hoover, H. 1944. Address to the twenty-third Republican National Convention, Chicago, June 17.

Horace. 1997. *The Odes of Horace.* Trans. D. Ferry. New York: Farrar, Straus & Giroux.

Horney, K. 1932. Dread of women. *International Journal of Psychoanalysis* 13:348–60.

Hrdy, S. B. 1981. *The Woman That Never Evolved.* Cambridge, Mass.: Harvard University Press.

Huntington, S. P. 1993. The clash of civilizations. *Foreign Affairs* 72 (Summer): 22–49.

Hynes, S. 1991. *A War Imagined: The First World War and English Culture.* New York: Atheneum.

Hynes, S. 1997. *The Soldiers' Tale: Bearing Witness to Modern War.* New York: Penguin.

Ikle, F. C. 1991. *Every War Must End.* New York: Columbia University Press.

Jacoby, S. 1983. *Wild Justice: The Evolution of Justice.* New York: Harper & Row.

James, W. 1911a. The moral equivalent of war. *Memories and Studies,* 267–96. Lecture 11. New York: Longman.

James, W. 1911b. Remarks at the peace banquet. *Memories and Studies,* 299–306. Lecture 12. New York: Longman.

Jerome, J. 1994. Low blows. *New York Times Magazine,* September 11.

Jones, J. 1962. *The Thin Red Line.* New York: Scribner.

Junger, E. 1929. *Storm of Steel.* Trans. from German. London: Chatto & Windus.

Keane, T., R. Zimering, and J. Caddell. 1985. A behavioral formulation of post traumatic stress disorder in Viet Nam veterans. *Behavior Therapist* 8:9–12.

Keegan, J. 1975. *The Face of Battle.* Toronto: Viking Penguin.

Keegan, J. 1995. *The Battle for History: Re-fighting World War II.* New York: Vintage.

Keegan, J. 2000. *The First World War.* New York: Vintage Books.

Kelleher, M.D., and C. L. Kelleher. 1998. *Murder Most Rare: The Female Serial Killer.* Westport, Conn.: Praeger.

Kerasote, T. 1993. *Bloodties: Nature, Culture and the Hunt.* New York: Random House.

Kipling, R. 1915. *Soldiers Three /The Story of the Gadsbys /In Black and White.* New York: Doubleday.

Kofoed, L., and J. Macmillan. 1989. Darwinian evolution of social behavior: Implications for group psychotherapy. *Psychiatry* 52:475–81.

Kojeve, A. 1991. *Introduction to the Reading of Hegel.* Trans. J. Nichols, Jr. Ithaca, N.Y.: Cornell University Press.

Krystal, J. H., S. M. Southwick, J. D. Bremner, and D. S. Charney. 1992. Emerging neurobiology of post-traumatic stress disorder. *Psychiatric Times,* August.

Kurtz, H. 1991. Correspondents chafe over curb on news. *Washington Post,* January 26.

Ladowsky, E. 1992. The gun club. *New Republic,* August 10.

MacArthur, D. 1962. *Address at West Point.* Farewell speech given to the corps of cadets at West Point, May 12; www.west-point.org/real/macarthur_address.html, accessed September 15, 2004.

Macdonald, L. 1978. *They Called It Passchendaele.* London: Michael Joseph.

Macdonald, L. 1988. *1914.* New York: Atheneum.

Machiavelli, N. 1950. *Discourse on Livy/Niccolo Machiavelli.* Trans. J. C. Bondanella and P. Bondanella. New York: Oxford University Press.

MacLean, P. D. 1985. Brain evolution relating to family, play and the separation call. *Archives of General Psychiatry* 42:505–17.

Macoby, E., and C. Jacklin. 1974. *The Psychology of Sex Differences.* Stanford, Calif.: Stanford University Press.

Mailer, N. 1975. *The Fight.* Boston: Little, Brown.

Manchester, W. 1983. *Goodbye Darkness.* New York: Dell.

Marcinko, R., and J. Wiseman. 1993. *Rogue Warrior.* New York: Pocket Books.

Marshall, S.L.A. 1947. *Men against Fire.* New York: William Morrow.

Martinez, A. 2004. Coming to terms with the doublespeak of war. *Los Angeles Times,* September 6.

Masters, R. D., and M. T. McGuire, eds. 1993. *The Neurotransmitter Revolution: Serotonin Social Behavior and the Law.* Carbondale: Southern Illinois University Press.

Matthiessen, P. 1962. *Under the Mountain Wall: A Chronicle of Two Seasons in the Stone Age.* New York: Viking.

McDougall, W. 1997. Sex, lies, and infantry. *Commentary,* September 3.

McNamara, R. S., and B. Van de Mark. 1995. In *Retrospect: The Tragedy and Lessons of Vietnam.* New York: Times Books.

McNeill, W. H. 1982. *The Pursuit of Power: Technology, Armed Force and Society since A.D. 1000.* Chicago: University of Chicago Press.

Mead, M. 2001. *Male and Female.* New York: HarperCollins.

Milgram, S. 1963. Behavioral study of obedience. *Journal of Abnormal and Social Psychology* 67:371–78.

Moellenhoff, F., and A. Moellenhoff. 1978. *Why War? The Correspondence between Albert Einstein and Sigmund Freud.* Chicago: Chicago Institute for Psychoanalysis.

Moran, C.M.W. 1987. *The Anatomy of Courage.* Boston: Houghton Mifflin.

Morris, M. 1996. By force of arms: Rape, war, and military culture. *Duke Law Journal* 45 (4): 651–781.

Nadelson, T. 1992. Attachment to killing. *Journal of the Academy of Psychoanalysis* 20:130–41.

Niditch, S. 1993. *War in the Hebrew Bible: A Study in the Ethics of Violence.* New York: Oxford University Press.

Nietzsche, F. 1989. *Beyond Good and Evil.* Trans. W. Kaufmann. New York: Vintage Books.

Ninh, B. 1993. *The Sorrow of War.* New York: Pantheon.

Norris, J. 1988. *Serial Killers.* New York: Anchor.

Oates, J. C., and D. Halpern, eds. 1988. *Reading the Fights: On Boxing.* New York: Holt.

O'Brien, T. 1990. *The Things They Carried.* Boston: Houghton Mifflin.

O'Brien, T. 1994. *In the Lake of the Woods.* Boston: Houghton Mifflin.

O'Connell, R. 1989. *Of Arms and Men: A History of War, Weapons and Aggression.* New York: Oxford University Press.

Owen, W. 1963a. Arms and the boy. In *The Collected Poems of Wilfred Owen,* 43. London: Chatto & Windus.

Owen, W. 1963b. Dulce et decorum est. In *The Collected Poems of Wilfred Owen,* 55–56. London: Chatto & Windus.

Paine, T. 1791. *Rights of Man.* Repr., New York: Citadel Press, 1948.

Palmer, L. 1993. How to bandage a war. *New York Times Magazine,* November 7.

Payne, S. G. 1995. *A History of Fascism, 1914–1945.* Madison: University of Wisconsin Press.

Pearson, P. 1997. *When She Was Bad: Violent Women and the Myth of Innocence.* New York: Viking.

Peters, R. 1997. Constant conflict. *Parameters* 27 (2): 4–14.

Peters, R. 2002. Rolling back radical Islam. *Parameters* 32 (3): 4–16.

Pitman, R. K. 1989. Animal models of compulsive behavior. *Biological Psychiatry* 16:189–98.

Puller, L., Jr. 1991. *Fortunate Son.* New York: Grove Press.

Rosenblatt, R. 1994. A killer in the eye. *New York Times Magazine,* June 5.

Rush, N. 1991. *Mating.* New York: Knopf.

Saathof, G. B. 1995. In the hall of mirrors, one Kuwaiti's captive memories. *Mind and Human Interaction* 6 (4): 170–78.

Saint Augustine. 1958. *The City of God.* New York: Image.

Sajer, G. 1967. *Forgotten Soldier.* New York: Harper & Row.

Santayana, G. 1924. Soliloquy #25: Tipperary. In *Soliloquies in England.* New York: Scribner's.

Schama, S. 1995. *Memory and Landscape.* New York: Knopf.

Seabrook, J. 1997. Tackling the competition. *New Yorker,* Aug. 18.

Sereny, G. 1996. *Albert Speer: His Battle with Truth.* New York: Vintage Books.

Shakespeare, W. 1997a. *Anthony and Cleopatra.* In *The Complete Works of Shakespeare,* ed. D. Bevington, 1293–1345. 4th ed. Boston: Addison-Wesley.

Shakespeare, W. 1997b. *Henry V.* In *The Complete Works of Shakespeare,* ed. D. Bevington, 849–93. 4th ed. Boston: Addison-Wesley.

Shakespeare, W. 1997c. *Lear.* In *The Complete Works of Shakespeare,* ed. D. Bevington, 1167–1219. 4th ed. Boston: Addison-Wesley.

Shakespeare, W. 1997d. *Macbeth.* In *The Complete Works of Shakespeare,* ed. D. Bevington, 4th ed. Boston: Addison-Wesley.

Shakespeare, W. 1997e. *Othello.* In *The Complete Works of Shakespeare,* ed. D. Bevington. 4th ed. Boston: Addison-Wesley.

Shakespeare, W. 1997f. *Troillus and Cressida.* In *The Complete Works of Shakespeare,* ed. D. Bevington, 444–94. 4th ed. Boston: Addison-Wesley.

Shatan, C. 1977. Bogus manhood, bogus honor: surrender and transfiguration in the United States Marine Corps. *Psychoanalytic Quarterly* 64:584–610.

Sheehan, N. 1988. *A Bright Shining Lie.* New York: Vintage.

Sleeper, J. 1997. Toward an end of blackness. *Harpers,* May.

Speer, A. 1976. *Spandau: The Secret Diaries.* New York: Macmillan.

Stoller, R. J. 1986. *Perversion: The Erotic Form of Hatred.* Washington, D.C.: American Psychiatric Press.

Swank, R. L., and W. E. Marchand. 1946. Combat neurosis. *Archives of Neurology* 55:236–46.

Taylor, M. 1997. Letter: Homer's women. *New York Times Book Review,* February 16.

Terkel, S. 1991. *The Good War.* New York: Pantheon Books.

Terr, L. 1991. Childhood traumas: An outline and overview. *American Journal of Psychiatry* 148:10–20.

Theweleit, K. 1987 and 1989. *Male Fantasies.* 2 vols. Minneapolis: University of Minnesota Press.

Tierney, P. 2000. *Darkness in El Dorado: How Scientists and Journalists Devastated the Amazon.* New York: W. W. Norton.

Tiger, L. 1969. *Men in Groups.* New York: Random House.

Tillich, P. 1977. *The Socialist Decision.* New York: Harper & Row.

Van der Kolk, B. A. 1989. The compulsion to repeat trauma: Reenactment, revictimization and masochism. *Psychiatric Clinics of North America* 12:389–411.

Van der Kolk, B. A., M. Greenberg, H. Boyd, and J. Krystal. 1985. Inescapable shock, neurotransmitters, and addiction to trauma: toward a psychobiology of posttraumatic stress. *Biological Psychiatry* 20:314–25.

Verhovek, S. H. 1993. Hold a baby or hold that line. *New York Times,* October 20.

Waite, R.G.L. 1952. *Vanguard of Nazism: The Free Corps in Postwar Germany, 1918–1922.* Cambridge, Mass.: Harvard University Press.

Walzer, M. 1977. *Just and Unjust Wars.* New York: Basic Books.

Ward, G. C., R. Burns, and K. Burns. 1990. *The Civil War: An Illustrated History.* New York: Knopf.

Weil, S. 1985. *The Iliad: The Poem of Force.* Wallingford, Pa.: Pendle Hill.

Whiting, J., and B. Whiting. 1975. Aloofness and intimacy between husbands and wives. *Ethos* 3:183–207.

Wills, G. 1997. *John Wayne's America: The Politics of Celebrity.* New York: Simon & Schuster.

Wilson, E. O. 1978. *On Human Nature.* Cambridge, Mass.: Harvard University Press.

Winter, D. 1979. *Death's Men: Soldiers of the Great War.* New York: Penguin.

Wood, E. 1991. *On Being Wounded.* Golden, Colo.: Fulcrum.

Woodhouse, J. 1998. *Gabriele d'Annunzio: Defiant Archangel.* New York: Oxford University Press.

Woolf, V. 1963. *Three Guineas.* New York: Harvest Books.

Yeats, W. B. 1997a. Easter 1916. In *The Collected Works of W. B. Yeats,* 182–84. Vol. 1. New York: Scribner's.

Yeats, W. B. 1997b. Under Ben Bulben. In *The Collected Works of W. B. Yeats,* 334. Vol. 1. New York: Scribner's.

Yehuda, R., and A. C. McFarlane. 1995. Conflict between current knowledge about posttraumatic stress disorder and its original conceptual basis. *American Journal of Psychiatry* 152 (12): 1705–13.

Zahn, P. (for Aaron Brown). 2003. The flyboys. *CNN Presents,* October 19.

INDEX

African Americans, 84

aggression: appropriate use of, 85–86; and civilization, 155; countering of, 86; and de-individuation, 24; and evolution, 167, 168, 174n5; Freud on, 166–67; genetic disposition toward, 155, 161; by group, 23; as innate, 18, 19; male vs. female, 6, 7, 140, 155–57, 160–61; and manhood, 11, 155; and marriage, 13; in military training, 25–26; national, 8, 167; in peacetime, 8; and pornography, 133, 134; postwar, 72; rituals of, 13; and sexuality, 13, 16, 124, 132–33; and society, 19, 156–57; in sport, 4; and survival, 166. *See also* counterforce; dominance/mastery; violence

anxiety, 88, 91, 93. *See also* fear; hyperalertness

atrocity, 31, 58, 60, 67–70, 90, 161

Augustine, Saint, 40

Baden-Powell, Sir Robert, 8

Barker, Pat: *Ghost Road,* 100

Bible, 9, 13, 26, 38, 39, 64, 106, 111, 131, 145, 149, 150

Blake, William, 107

boyhood, 3–21, 160–61, 163

Boy Scout Movement, 8

brain, 84, 171n3

Brooke, Rupert, 107

Brownmiller, Susan, 153

Burbank, Victoria, 157

Buruma, Ian, 119

Campbell, Joseph, 66

Caputo, Philip, 111

Chagnon, Napoleon, 18, 145, 172n7

Churchill, Winston, 20, 83, 107, 108, 123

Citadel, The, 129

civilian, 24, 25–26, 57, 61, 167

civilization, 140; and aggression, 155; defense of, 169; evolution of, 44, 73, 167–68, 174n5; as innate, 19; Islamic fundamentalist, 162–63, 169; and killing, 43, 55, 73; law of, 82; and resistance to killing, 44; and restraint, 73; and violence, 160; women vs. men in, 144–45. *See also* society

Clausewitz, C. von, 44, 69–70, 93, 115, 131, 147, 149

commanding officer(s), 29, 43, 55, 60, 69, 72, 98, 99, 100, 141–42, 154

comrade, 22–34; and atrocity, 31, 60, 68, 161; bond with, 16, 52, 112, 116, 117, 120, 161; care for, 95–96; closeness to, 12; and death, 22, 23, 82, 93; and family, 28; in fascism, 151, 152; and fear, 28; and killing, 40–41, 72; loss of, 79; in military training, 25; and posttraumatic stress disorder, 91, 92; and psychological trauma, 90; and reenlistment, 30; and self-sacrifice, 30; self-sacrifice for, 28; and sexuality, 23, 27, 126, 127–29; survival with, 124; and veterans, 28; in war, 27; and wife, 28; and women, 150. *See also* group

Conroy, Pat: *The Lords of Discipline,* 129

contest, 3, 4, 5, 13, 14, 40, 78, 150

counterforce, 77–88, 91, 95. *See also* aggression

courage, 20–21, 34, 118

cowardice, 32–33. *See also* softness/weakness

danger, 33, 39, 43, 91

death: and athletes, 4; in Bible, 13; and comradeship, 22, 23, 82, 93; and cowardice, 33; escape from, 66; fear of, 43, 95, 117–18, 161; from friendly fire, 98–99; manhood at, 19; and men vs. women, 142, 143; mimicked in sport, 6; and posttraumatic stress disorder, 91, 94, 95; profundity of, 38; readiness for,

A person of wide-ranging interests from film to cooking to playing squash, Theodore Nadelson, M.D., was born in Brooklyn, New York, in 1930. A veteran of both the Alaskan Wildlife Service and the U.S. Army, he trained as a psychiatrist and psychoanalyst, developing a specific expertise in mental health issues affecting soldiers and veterans. Having experienced military life himself, he could share with other veterans a deep sense of understanding, comradeship, and devotion. Veterans found it easy to expose their demons to him, and they felt strengthened by his genuine interest and concern.

During his professional career, he served as a faculty member of Harvard, Tufts, and Boston University medical schools. He was an outstanding clinician, a superb teacher, and a respected scholar. His distinguished career began as a consultant to the medical and surgical services of the Beth Israel Hospital in Boston, Massachusetts. As chief of psychiatry at the Boston Veterans Administration Hospital for twenty years, he endeared himself to students, to faculty, and to patients. In this role, he encountered the many veterans who inspired this book. He talked with them about their war experiences and videotaped these meetings, sharing and discussing these tapes with the veterans and with his students.

Beginning this book in the late 1980s, he painstakingly wove the stories he heard from veterans into his study of the psychology, history, and literature of war and killing, enlivening his work with literary references and historical accounts.

Ted Nadelson passed away in October 2003, leaving behind his wife, Carol, whose career he fostered and supported; his children, Robert and Jennifer, to whom he imparted his wit and love of life; and his granddaughter, Sarah.